CONCILIUM

Religion in the Seventies

CONCILIUM

Concilium 119 (9/1978): Spirituality

DISCERNMENT OF THE SPIRIT AND OF SPIRITS

Edited by

Casiano Floristán and Christian Duquoc

A CROSSROAD BOOK

The Seabury Press · New York

1979
The Seabury Press
815 Second Avenue
New York, N.Y. 10017

Library of Congress Catalog Card Number: 79-83935
ISBN: 0-8164-0409-7
ISBN: 0-8164-2199-4 (pbk.)
Printed in the United States of America

CONTENTS

Part III
Christian Life Today

Part IV
Bulletins

Part V
Conclusion

Editorial

THE Ritual of Penance states that discernment is the 'intimate aware-ness of the action of God in the heart of men, the gift of the Holy Spirit and the fruit of love'. It is not surprising that discretion should be related to personal conversion and communal reconciliation. Dis-cernment and discretion are something other than just understanding, interpreting; they have to do with the transformation of man. We live in a society much given to the practice of criticism. We hear a lot in many quarters of interpretation, hermeneutics, evaluation, the 'final bal-ance,' analysis, revision and self-criticism. Spiritual discernment is an ancient and profound tradition in Christian spirituality, and is clearly related to the kingdom of God. The discernment of spirits is a prophetic task. Hence the importance of the criteria of discernment in Israel.

The discernment of spirits was described in a characteristic and unique way by Ignatius in his Spiritual Exercises. Ignatius of Loyola is, in fact, the great master of the practice of discernment. The instances of Christian discernment that followed him owe much to his example. Nevertheless we should not forget the contributions of the modern masters of analysis, above all Marx and Freud, to this complex of questions. They help us in our task of discernment with a clarified religious awareness.

This *Concilium* reveals the authors' understanding that Christian discernment is not to be restricted to the spiritual or interior life; that its ultimate objective is to realize in actuality the kingdom of God; that it is a complete and overall process which depends on concrete situa-tions, historical attachments and psychological conditions; that Chris-tian discernment depends on a clear option for the poor and the op-pressed; that Christian discernment demands great openness to the action of the Spirit; that the subject of discernment is the people of God in a state of communion with the Church; that discernment is a funda-mental choice, a prophetic task, a practical decision, virtue and charism. It demands a human interpretative model and an evangelical programme of action leading to the actual realization of the kingdom of God.

CHRISTIAN DUQUOC
CASIANO FLORISTÁN

In Memory of
Father Albert-Marie Besnard

INSTEAD of the article Father Besnard was asked for—he has died in the meantime—we reproduce the substance of a letter intended for his brethren and his friends 'in case of an unexpected departure for Jerusalem—the Jerusalem up there . . .' The letter was given to us by Professor Jean-Claude Sagne.

'I should like you to know that I am ready, if to be ready is not to have reached a certain degree of perfection but to have understood in my very bones that my poor life is nothing other than what God may wish it to be when of his mercy I can simply lay it between the palms of his hands. That is rather wonderful. Finally I shall be able to love with the very Heart of God. A marvellous thing to contemplate. At last I am going to be useful to the Church. At last I am going to live Life's very movement and lightness.

'I say simply that I should like to live my life over again, because only now am I at last beginning to be a follower of the Gospel in my heart and to begin to feel a certain Word whispering in me. I should like to have borne witness more effectively, to have woven with others this cloth of friendship and understanding in the service of the less advantaged. But peace—others will do that, others will say those words.

'It is true that I have often felt alone in the inexperience of faith that was my lot. I thought I sensed (perhaps I was right, perhaps wrong, I don't know, God knows) something like a reawakening of the living God, of the Father of Jesus Christ in our world—Another way of seeing everything that God has prepared for his Son through the infinite dimension of the universe and humanity . . .

'I do not have time to express what I should have liked to say for the pure pleasure of those who are close to me in friendship. It doesn't matter. The words that the Word emits in the silence of the communion he establishes between all men contains all that we would wish to say or shout to all people and what all the books in the world could never hold.

'Return in peace to your life and to your everyday tasks, just as in peace I cross the threshold of the House where we shall all meet. I have loved Jerusalem so much.'

The life of a faithful Christian, when it is spent under the impress of the Spirit, is a song of love with a special theme. The life of Albert Besnard was such a song expressing the desire to rediscover the countenance of the Father.

CHRISTIAN DUQUOC
CASIANO FLORISTÁN

PART I

The Bible

Martin McNamara

Discernment Criteria in Israel:
True and False Prophets

IT IS recognized that the discernment of spirits is one of the most difficult arts in the guidance of men and Churches. This has been so down through the centuries and seems to be more so today. The greater the emphasis on the charismatic element in the community, the more keenly is the need for discernment felt. It is only natural that today those concerned with the problem should turn to the pages of the Old and New Testaments for guidance. In this essay I shall devote our attention to some aspects of the question in the Old Testament.[1]

PROPHECY OUTSIDE ISRAEL

In the Old Testament the term prophet (in Hebrew *nabî*) is not reserved for those whom both we and Hebrew tradition regarded as true or classical prophets. The Old Testament uses the same term to designate a much larger group of persons: members of prophetic guilds, court prophets, a larger group with whom the true prophets were often in conflict, false prophets, worshippers of Yahweh, the God of Israel, but also prophets of false gods, e.g., Astarte (1 Kg. 18:19) or Baal, the god of Canaan (1 Kg. 18:19, 22 etc.; 2 Kg. 10:19). From this evidence it would appear that the Canaanites used this same term as a designation for their own prophets. That this was so is confirmed by Jeremiah 27:2, 9 which says that the kings of Edom, Moab, Ammon, Tyre and Sidon

3

had for consultation *prophets* (*nebî'îm*), diviners, dreamers, sooth-sayers and sorcerers. The very Hebrew word for prophet (*nabî*) is a loan-word, not a native Hebrew one, further evidence of the foreign roots of the phenomenon of prophecy. So far it has not been attested in a Canaanite language outside of the Bible and in the Hebrew Lachish letters from the time of Jeremiah. Despite this we can presume it was in use among the pagan Canaanites and probably in Ibla (near present-day Aleppo) before patriarchal times. In the texts recently found there (dating from about 2400–2250 B.C.) one of the two classes of prophets known in that city was called *nabi'ūtum*,[2] a term related to the Hebrew *nabî*.

A further reminder of the pagan roots of the phenomenon can be found in the term 'prophet' itself. It has come into modern languages through Latin from Greek. For the early pagan Greeks, prophet and associated words denoted appointed men and women and their work, which was to declare something believed not to be derived from themselves but from the god who revealed his will at a particular site. In ancient Greece an oracle prophet proclaimed the will and counsel of the god in answer to questions and with reference to the particular situation of the person who sought advice.[3]

This desire to ascertain the will of the gods and to foretell future events is natural to those who believe in a divine being. We have ample evidence from ancient texts that the nations around Israel (with the possible exception of Ancient Egypt) had both men and women who were prophets, diviners and such like, mainly professional. These purported to foretell the future and communicate the will of a deity to certain persons, mainly kings. Prophecy in the ancient city of Mari (eighteenth century B.C.) is a favourite topic of study for present-day scholars. The recent Ibla finds will probably provide material for a similar study for a much earlier period. We have an interesting Aramaic text from Zakir, king of Hamath, to the north of Israel, from about 780–775 B.C (shortly before the time of Amos and Isaiah), in which the king tells us that in answer to his prayer, his god Baalshamayn answered him through seers (*ḥazayn*) and messengers (or diviners).[4] These were probably his court prophets, and the Aramaic word for seer is the same as one of the two Hebrew terms used to designate the persons also known as prophets.

PROPHECY IN ISRAEL

The nations surrounding Israel and their kings might have their prophets, diviners, dreamers, soothsayers, and sorcerers (cf. Jer. 27:9). With Israel matters were different. She was the chosen people of the living God, who spoke once directly on the mountain of revelation and would continue to communicate his will through a succession of prophets. 'There shall not be found among you . . . any one who practises divination,[5] a soothsayer or an augur, or a sorcerer, or a charmer, or a medium, or a wizard, or a necromancer. For whoever does these things is an abomination to the Lord . . . For these nations, which you are about to dispossess, give heed to soothsayers and diviners; but as for you, the Lord your God has not allowed you to do' (Dt. 18:10–14). Israel had no need of these since she had instead the living voice of prophecy, in a succession of prophets like Moses himself. 'The Lord your God will raise up for you a prophet like me (Moses), from your brethren—him you shall heed' (Dt. 18:15).

This belief is older than our present book of Deuteronomy. Isaiah laments that the people consult the dead, mediums and wizards, instead of their God (Is. 8:18–20), who had spoken through Isaiah himself. Through the prophet Moses, God had brought Israel from Egypt and had spoken his word to her through prophets, raised up by him in succession to Moses (cf. Hos. 12:13; Am. 2:10–11). These we may describe as charismatic prophets. There were others in Israel, however, who are called prophets in the Bible, but without much, if any, evidence that they had received a special divine vocation. The prophetic groups, called 'sons of the prophets' which appeared during the age of Samuel and continued into later times were often characterized by 'ecstatic' or frenetic behaviour. This trait they had in common with Canaanite pagan prophets, from whom they differed of course by reason of their devotion to Yahweh, the God of Israel. In fact these groups were in later times passionate devotees of strict Yahwehism against the incursions of Canaanite religion. Then there were royal prophets and court prophets. God is called both a prophet and David's seer (2 Sam. 24:11). In 1 Samuel 22:5 he gives counsel to David as a pagan seer would give to his king. We read that Ahab, king of Israel, had in his entourage about four hundred prophets, of whom he enquired ('the word of the Lord') whether or not he should go to battle with Syria or not (1 Kg. 22:5–28). This consultation of the Lord through the prophets was a legitimate and accepted practice in Israel. These prophets of Ahab's court were believed to have been able to communicate 'the word of the Lord'. In practice they were 'yes-men', and gave a favourable reply—all except one, Micaiah ben Imlah. His dissenting voice led to a conflict with the spokesman for the others as to who really had the word of the Lord. One can legitimately ask to what extent such court prophets were really 'raised up by God'.

Then there were other prophets, often mentioned in conjunction with the priests and apparently in some way connected with public worship in the temple or local sanctuaries. On a number of occasions some of these were in conflict with the great prophets (e.g., Isaiah, Micah, Jeremiah), who refer to them as 'prophets of lies', false prophets. They probably believed that they were genuine prophets through whom the Lord delivered his word to the people. In a number of instances this was probably the case, but they often appear to have been no more than self-deluded individuals.

Prophecy in Israel was, then, a rather complex phenomenon, by reason of its larger pre-history and the intervention of God in the life of his people through Moses and the messengers raised up by God in succession to Moses. It was evident that certain criteria were required for the discernment of true prophecy from false, both on the part of both prophet and people.

CRITERIA OF TRUE AND FALSE PROPHETS

Genuine Prophecy a Divine Gift

It is clear that biblical tradition regards prophecy as a gift of God to his people. It was so regarded by Amos (2:10–11), and Hosea (12:13) at the beginnings of the period of classical prophecy in Israel, and this belief would remain constant in later times. Through prophecy, the God who had once spoken through Moses would continue to direct his people (Dt. 18:15–18). According to Jeremiah 6:17 the prophets were set by God as watchmen, sentries for the people; Ezekiel had the same mission for the individual Israelite (Ezek. 3:17–19; 33:7–9). As watchman or sentry the prophet had the task of seeing impending moral danger and alerting the people. Jeremiah was appointed by God an assayer of his people (Jer. 6:27), to test and assay their conduct, to evaluate its worth and make their standing in God's sight plain to them.

Moral Obligation to Heed the True Prophet

The prophets of Israel had a mission in a very definite context. They were sent to God's covenanted people to remind them of the nature and demands of their election by God, to guide this people through the vicissitudes of its history, by condemnation, exhortation or consolation as occasion demanded. Prophecy for Israel was the living voice of the reality of their God and of the covenant. It followed that Israel was not free to reject the teaching of God's messengers. Moses is presented as saying concerning the prophet like himself which God would raise up for Israel: 'I shall put my words in his mouth and he shall speak all that I command him. And whoever will not give heed to my words which he shall speak in my name, I myself will require it of him' (Dt. 18:18–19; cf. also Ezek. 3:19; 33:9).

If it was a serious matter to ignore the words of a prophet, it follows that to assume the role of prophet without being sent by God was more so. Deuteronomy 18:20 goes so far as to say that a prophet who presumptuously preaches in Yahweh's name without having a divine commission, or who prophesies in the name of other gods, 'shall die', presumably by execution for apostasy (cf. Dt. 13:5).

Although the teaching on prophecy as formulated in the book of Deuteronomy comes from a later period, its substance can be assumed to have held good for Israelite prophecy during the classical one.

The Reality of False Prophecy

We know relatively little of false prophecy in Israel before the period of the great independent prophetic figures from the time of Elijah onwards. False prophets or prophets 'prophesying' what the people or kings wanted to hear, probably already existed. The problem, however, became highlighted only with the advent of the great independent prophets when conflicts arise between the institutional prophets of the older order and the newer classical prophets who had a clear consciousness of having been sent by God.

Elijah's conflict was with the prophets of Baal who had been introduced by Jezebel, the wife of King Ahab of Israel, in the ninth century and had the support of her husband. Ahab himself had a band of about four hundred prophets, as we have noted already. These were Yahwistic prophets, but gave to the king as the word of God what his majesty wanted to hear. Micaiah ben Imlah was another court prophet, but was known for his unfavourable replies. Once when summoned to give his reply, and having been forewarned that all the other prophets had given a favourable one, Micaiah answered: 'As the Lord lives, what the Lord says to me, that will I speak' (1 Kg. 22:13–14). He then recounted his vision from the Lord which was one of disaster for the king. The Lord, Micaiah continues, had put a lying spirit in the mouths of the other prophets in order to deceive Ahab; these prophets, in fact, had really spoken evil concerning the king (1 Kg. 22:17–23).

Isaiah (28:7) had strong words on the priests and prophets of Ephraim who reeled with strong drink, erred in (prophetic) vision and stumbled in giving judgment. His contemporary Micah had similar words against the prophets of Judah who were leading the people astray, preaching that all would be well ('peace'), and apparently tailoring their oracles to the gratuity offered (Mic. 3:5–8, 11). It was such prophets, in any case, that the people wanted to have (Mic. 2:6, 11).

Both Micah (3:6–7, 11) and Isaiah (3:2) link prophet and diviner. It may be that the prophets of their age gave oracles through some form of divination.

The activity of these 'institutional' prophets was particularly pronounced during the ministry of Jeremiah. They are generally mentioned together with priests and may have been connected with the temple service. The question of true and false prophet was particularly acute in Jeremiah's day in that some at least of these other prophets were preaching the exact opposite of Jeremiah's message as the word of the Lord and using symbolic actions to stress their point, just as Jeremiah did (cf. Jer., ch. 28). The activity of these opponents of God's messengers was equally in evidence among the Jewish exiles in Babylon during the same period (Jer. 29:1, 8, 15, 21, 32). Ezekiel, in part Jeremiah's contemporary, had also to contend with their pernicious activity (Ezek. 13:2–16; 22:23).

A criterion for distinguishing between true and false prophet was clearly called for.

The Prophet's Criterion

In the case of the classical prophets of the Old Testament, their charismatic experience of God at their vocation and later seems to have been self-authenticating. It appears to have left them in no doubt that they had encountered God, that they had 'stood in the council (sôd) of the Lord', that they had been given a knowledge of his secret plan for his people and had been sent as messengers to bear his word to Israel. In the light of this vision and experiences they judged the people, its princes, priests and the other prophets. We read of this encounter with God in the prophetic writings. 'The Lord has spoken' says Amos (3:8), 'who can but prophesy?' Jeremiah felt the power of the prophetic word within him as a burning coal, an inner compulsion to prophesy (Jer. 20:7–10). The prophets with whom these charismatic messengers of God were in conflict did not have this special experience of God, nor were they sent by him. Speaking of these other prophets the Lord says: 'For who among them has stood in the council (sôd) of the Lord to perceive and hear his word, or who has given heed to his word and listened?' (Jer. 23:18). 'I did not send these prophets, yet they ran; I did not speak to them, yet they prophesied. But if they had stood in my council, then they would have proclaimed my words to my people, and they would have turned them from the evil of their doings' (Jer. 23:21–22). Their encounter with God gave the true prophets an awareness of God's nature, of his plan for his people and of the moral demands that made the divine election of Israel. It also gave the prophets the moral endowments required to proclaim the divine message in the face of adversity and opposition. Contrasting his own person and message with those of the false prophets, Micah (3:8) says: 'But as for me, I am filled with power . . . and justice and might, to declare to Jacob his transgression and to Israel his sin'.

In pre-exilic times, the charismatic prophets were, by and large, prophets of doom, the burden of their message being that the people's sinfulness would bring divine punishment and national disaster (Not, of course, that their message was entirely one of doom; Isaiah, for instance, prophesied that Jerusalem would be saved from destruction; cf. Is. 37:23–29, 33–34). A frequent accusation of these prophets against their prophetic opponents was that they preached 'peace': that all would be well with God's people (cf. Mic. 3:5, 11; Jer. 23:17; 6:14; Ezek, 13:3–16). They are accused of preaching the visions of their own hearts as God's word.

A prophet, whether charismatic or otherwise, had to see to it that he did not take his own desires as divine revelation. 'Let a prophet who has a dream, tell his dream, but let him who has my word speak my word faithfully. What has straw in common with wheat says the Lord' (Jer. 23:28). His initial encounter with God would have given the true prophet a conviction of his prophetic vocation and, apparently, the insight to judge on the demands made by God's law. It did not empower him, however, to give divine replies on particular cases at will. Once Jeremiah had to await ten days for a divine reply (Jer. 42:2–7). On another occasion Jeremiah was confronted by the prophet Hananiah who, contrary to Jeremiah's preaching, was proclaiming as God's word that the power of Nebuchadnezzar, king of Babylon and master of Judah, would soon be destroyed and Judah saved. Although, on the analogy of earlier prophecy, Jeremiah surmised that Hananiah was wrong, only on receipt of a direct message from God did he declare him to be a false prophet (Jer. 28:1–16).

By what criteria, we may ask, could Hananiah and the many other false prophets come to realize that they were mere victims of hallucination? By Jeremiah's time there was a certain validity in the argument from earlier prophecy. The earlier prophets, by then recognized as genuine, had prophesied divine chastisement (cf. Jer. 28:8). This criterion, however, was not universally valid. The voice of the earlier prophets was not univocal. Micah had predicted that Jerusalem would be destroyed (Mic. 3:12), whereas Isaiah, his contemporary, had said it would be spared. Prophecy, however, was not concerned merely with prediction. The demands made by the divine election of Israel, and by traditional covenant law were binding, and knowledge of them required no charismatic experience. The false prophets appear to have failed to preach these demands. The source of their deception probably lay in their own personal religious lives. They lacked that communion with God of which Psalm 25.11 speaks: 'The friendship (*sôd*) of the Lord is for those who fear him, and he makes known to them his covenant'. Because of this they failed to distinguish between their own dreams and God's word. A knowledge of the divine transcendence would have made them aware of the gravity of this.

Ultimately, then, it would appear that by reason of the nature of prophecy, the genuiness of which depends on an internal experience, no objective norm can be given, although there were criteria which could help the prophet realize that he had not been sent by God. We must admit, however, that we know far too little of the complex problem of prophecy in ancient Israel to go beyond this minimum. In between the great prophets on the one hand and the charlatans on the other, there must have been many of whom we know little or nothing.

Criteria for the People

Although the people were bound by religious obligation to follow the true prophet and reject the false one (Dt. 18:18–22), it does not appear that there were any clear criteria enabling the people to distinguish between the two. There are, however, certain rudimentary norms. Apart from these the problem of discernment had, it would appear, to be confronted and answered for each individual occasion as it arose. Here we shall now consider criteria given or presupposed in the Old Testament, almost all of which are concerned with the discernment of false, not of true, prophecy.

(a) *Orthodoxy and inducement to apostasy.* Deuteronomy 13:1–5 considers prophecy in the context of laws dealing with enticement to idolatry or apostasy. Even though the predictions of a prophet inducing to idolatry ('going after other gods') should come true, the prophet in question was none the less a false one and was to be put to death. The criterion employed is that of fidelity to the central truth of Israelite religion. The norm holds good for the limited case for which the context intends it. If extended to include fidelity to the national religion it could endanger the lives of the genuine prophets, who at times spoke out boldly against public worship, the temple (Mic. 3:12; Jer. 7:14; 26:1–23), the very existence of the nation and even the Mosaic covenant (cf. Jer. 31:31–34). It was possibly some such interpretation of this criterion which almost cost Jeremiah his life (Jer. 26:11).

(b) *Fulfilment of prophecy.* What at first sight looks like a universal norm for discernment is given in Deuteronomy 18:20–2. 'The prophet who presumes to speak a word in my name which I have commanded him to speak, or who speaks in the name of other gods, that same prophet shall die. And if you say in your heart, "How may we know the word which the Lord has spoken?"—When the prophet speaks in the name of the Lord, if the word does not come to pass or not come true, that is a word which the Lord has not spoken; the prophet has spoken it presumptuously, you need not be afraid of him'. The principle of non-fulfilment as a sign that a prophet was not sent by God was invoked regarding his own person by Micaiah ben Imlah (1 Kg. 22:28) and that of the prophet who spoke presumptuously dying was verified in the case of Hananiah (Jer. 28:16–17).

The criterion, however, is of very limited utility and of value only when restricted to the time of the prophet and his contemporaries. It ignores the principle given in Jeremiah 18:7–10, viz. that some prophecies, although formulated absolutely, are in God's mind subject to man's response with regard to their fulfilment. A further difficulty regarding the criterion is that the time of fulfilment of a prophecy is subject to the divine good pleasure and no time limit can be set (cf. 2 Pet. 3:2–9). Jeremiah himself was acutely embarrassed by the delay in the fulfilment of his prophecies (cf. Jer. 17:15). While many of the earlier prophecies were fulfilled in Israel's own history, others were not, causing anguish to pious reflective minds (cf. Dan. 9:2, 24–27; Sir. [Ec.] 36:14–16). Finally, even fulfilment of a prediction is not in itself proof that the person who made it is a genuine prophet (cf. Dt. 13:1–3).

(c) *Contents of the preaching: woe or welfare.* The pre-exilic classical prophets accused the other prophets of leading the people astray by preaching 'peace, peace' when there was no peace (Jer. 6:14), whereas the message of the true prophets tended to be one of impending doom. Jeremiah himself, as we have seen, invoked this criterion of the analogy of prophecy in his altercation with Hananiah (Jer. 28:8). The courage to go against popular sentiment, particularly when accompanied by outspoken teaching on the demands of the covenant, should have constituted for the people a *prima facie* case that such prophets were genuine, and pandering to the whims of the populace should have created a suspicion of insincerity. However, this norm too is of limited value. It would have been useful only in certain circumstances. Not all pre-exilic prophecy was prediction of disaster, and from later exilic times onwards (the later Ezekiel, Second Isaiah, and so on) prophecy concentrated mainly on consolation and encouragement.

(d) *Moral life of the prophet.* The classical prophets often speak disparagingly of the moral behaviour of their prophetic opponents.

They ply their trade through the land (Jer. 14:18), leading the people astray. They are sometimes accused of false dealing (Jer. 6:13), of drunkenness (Is. 28:7), of prophesying or divining for money (Mic. 3:5, 11), of using other prophets' oracles (Jer. 23:30). These accusations, however, were hardly intended as a criterion of prophecy as such. They are directed against immoral behaviour and sometimes the strictures are directed against both priest and prophet together (Is. 28:7; Jer. 6:13–14; 14:18).

While flagrant immoral behaviour can be a solid indication that a prophet has not been sent by God (although God can prophesy through immoral persons; cf. Mt. 7:22), moral behaviour in itself is no sure criterion of genuine prophecy or orthodoxy. Holy people can be subject to self-deception.

(e) *Discernment and personal living faith.* The criteria so far considered concern the discernment of false prophets. Consideration of their insufficiency might give the impression that in practice Israel had no means of discerning true prophet from false, or of recognizing the true prophet whose words the people were obliged to heed (Dt. 18:18–19). Such an inference would be mistaken. The criteria considered have to do mainly with prophecy considered as prediction. The mission of the true prophet, however, went far beyond this and was concerned with Israel's total relationship with her God. Prophecy within God's people was an aspect of the covenant. It belonged to the realm of faith. By reason of the nature of the case, a living faith, an openness to God, and his activity in history, to his word, are required in order to recognize his messengers. Without such faith no criterion, however strong, is convincing. The biblical evidence indicates that only too often Israel lacked these basic requirements and in consequence, instead of accepting the prophets raised up for her by God created and sustained a moral climate where prophets of her own liking could flourish. Jeremiah (Jer. 5:30–31) could lament: 'An appalling and horrible thing has happened in the land: the prophets prophesy falsely, and the priests rule at their direction; *my people love to have it so'*. God had earlier said through Amos (2:11–2): 'I raised up some of your sons for prophets, and some of your young men for Nazirites . . . But you made the Nazirites drink wine, and you commanded the prophets, saying, "You shall not prophesy" '. The popular response to Micah's outspoken preaching was: ' "Do not preach . . . One should not preach of such things; disgrace will not overtake us" ' (Mic. 2:6). Micah's own comment is: 'If a man should go about and utter wind and lies, saying, "I will preach to you of wine and strong drink," he would be the preacher for this people' (Mic. 2:11; cf. also Jer. 44:15–19).

Some of the 'prophets of doom' were forewarned by God to be prepared to meet opposition and have their message rejected (cf. Is. 6:9–13; Jer. 1:17–19; 15:19–20; Ezek. 2:3–7). Faith, however, was also required for the acceptance of prophecies of consolation. Second Isaiah spoke of the glorious future God had in store for his people. He knew, however, that Israel could come into possession of the promises only through faith and conversion and at the close of his work calls for this conversion (Is. 55:6–8). God's thoughts and ways are beyond those of men (Is. 55:8–9).

The prophets have revealed his word and his plan of salvation which will ultimately triumph (Is. 55:10–11). Only through faith can this free gift of God be accepted in any age. It is no easy matter to discern who at any given time is a genuine spokesman for God's plan, but discernment must be made in the light of the broad context of the divine mystery of salvation, now finally revealed in Christ, but intended to be ever more deeply understood and lived under the guidance of the Holy Spirit, the Spirit who spoke through the prophets of old and continues to make God's word a living reality.

Notes

1. *See* W. Vogels, 'Comment discerner le prophète authentique?', *Nouvelle Revue Théologique* 99 (1977), pp. 681–701 (with further literature); A. S. Van der Woude, 'Micah in Dispute with the Pseudo-Prophets', *Vetus Testamentum* 19 (1969), pp. 244–60; J. Lindblom, *Prophecy in Ancient Israel* (Oxford, 1963), pp. 29–32, 47–104, 210–15.

2. See G. Pettinato, *Biblical Archaeologist* 39 (1976), p. 49.

3. Cf. H. Kramer, *Theological Dictionary of the New Testament*, vol. VI, p. 791 (*Theologisches Wörterbuch zum Neuen Testament, VI*, 1959, pp. 790–91).

4. For original text and translation see C. L. Gibson, *Textbook of Syrian Semitic Inscriptions*, vol. 2 (Oxford, 1975), pp. 6–17; translations also in J. B. Pritchard, ed., *Ancient Near Eastern Texts* (1955), p. 501; D. Winton Thomas ed., *Documents from Old Testament Times* (Edinburgh, 1958; New York, 1961), p. 247.

5. It is not quite clear in what precise sense divination is to be understood in this text. It is linked with prophecy in Is. 3:2; Mic. 3:7, without apparent condemnation of the practice as such; cf. also Ezek. 13.7.

Jon Sobrino

Following Jesus as Discernment

BY Christian discernment I understand the particular quest for the will of God, not only to understand it but also to carry it out. Discernment is therefore to be understood not only literally but as a process in which the will of God carried out also verifies the will of God thought.

I have been asked to develop the theme from the basis of Christology since traditional ecclesiology does not seem to offer an adequate response to the radical challenge posed to Christian life conceived as discernment in the sense I have applied it. While the traditional structures of ecclesial existence seemed to offer a sufficiently Christian channel for the will of God to be known and practiced on the basis of the inertia of living in this channel, the present-day Church—at least in many parts of the world—is looking for a real incarnation and particular mediations of Christian life which cannot be deduced from the inertia of the old structures. The urgency of the task requires not vague determinations of what is good or bad, but the quest for the particular act which truth requires to be performed. Insistence in some parts on the eschatological reserve, which is necessary in its way, is not sufficient to incarnate the Christian in the world of today; and it has its dangerous side, since the problem of discernment does not end with de-absolutizing the particular historical context, but in meeting the particular context of what has to be done according to Paul's requirement of a love that moves us on.

What this setting of the question means is that we have to overcome the simply ethical understanding of Christianity based on doing good and avoiding evil and progress to a seriously theological questioning of the meaning of the Christian task. With the problem posed in this way, the title of this article should be clear, although on this point—as on other points—many Christologies have not made it so. If being Christian means becoming sons in the Son, then Christian discernment must have a structure similar to the discernment of Jesus, which can only be achieved by following him. The only thing that needs clarification and not presupposition is in what Jesus' discernment consisted, so that our following of him can be discernment in truth.

More basically, however, the title of the article should not be clear if it implies a mechanical imitation of the process Jesus went through, since this—besides being impossible—would be a denial of the need for discernment at the present time. This is the moment to call on the Spirit of Jesus in which we have to carry on discerning. The only thing that needs clarifying is that this Spirit should be in truth the Spirit of Jesus and not presupposed as existing, already institutionalized in ecclesial structures, or spontaneously in the various versions of pentecostalism and the charismatic movement. This has to be verified starting from Jesus, not declared *a priori* as the possession of an institution or a gift to particular groups. If we pose the problem of Christian discernment in the tension between the history of Jesus and the history unfolded by his Spirit, we will not be able to offer simple recipes even from Jesus. What I am trying to put forward is the *structure* of Jesus' discernment, which should be recreated throughout history according to the Spirit of Jesus, and this can only be done by starting from a trinitarian reality as opposed to a mere concept of the trinity.

THE FATHER OF JESUS AS REQUIREMENT AND POSSIBILITY OF DISCERNMENT FOR JESUS

Speaking of the trinitarian reality which Christian discernment requires means approaching it from the real history of Jesus.[1] In this sense, the first and basic statement to be made is that not any understanding of the divinity requires us to discern if we are to obtain an idea of what it means. If the Father of Jesus had been the pure rationality of creation or its intrinsic morality, an absolute hypostasized as reason, power or love, then Jesus would not have needed to discern. For Jesus, discerning the will of God meant at first nothing other than clarifying for himself who God really is. This process of clarification gradually made clear to Jesus both the reality of God and the need to discern. We can call this first relationship between Jesus and God the first discernment on the basis of which the structure and contents of his particular discernments will become understandable.

We know, because we can deduce from the Gospels, that Jesus

began his activity with the consciousness of a Jew who had received the best traditions concerning God, stemming from the history of his people. Jesus appeared to sum up these traditions in the tradition that called God the God of the kingdom, and it was to be the quest for the particular will of God concerning this kingdom that God was to appear to him in the first place as an *always greater God.*

In his announcement and initiation of the kingdom of God, Jesus came to realize that the tradition received, including that of the will of God as expressed in the Old Testament, is neither absolute nor definitive. Despite his previous knowledge of God, Jesus came to feel that no tradition of God and none of the possible structures of the kingdom were final and definitive, providing an unequivocal channel for finding the will of God. The temptations in the desert, the crisis in Galilee, the prayer in the garden and his death on the cross, all provide examples of this growing experience in discernment.

Jesus always saw the need to examine the will of God concerning the kingdom and indirectly concerning himself. A will that went beyond the limits of what was already known as good and was posited as something particular and new that he had to be and to do. From this point of view, the story of the temptations of Jesus, which the Evangelists attached so much importance to, is nothing other than the story of the dialogue between Jesus and his Father on how to do the right thing with his novel and sovereign liberty and in this way also with the very reality of the Father.

In the history of the real consciousness of Jesus, the God of the Jewish traditions then appeared to him with a formality that Jesus took absolutely seriously: God is always greater but this transcendence of God does not appear basically in distancing himself from creation but in questioning and through creation. The primary need to discern was seen by Jesus along with his discovery of the greater being of God. The objective reality of an always greater God is matched by his subjective attitude of allowing God to be God. 'Discerning' and 'the greater God' then become corresponding realities that are only clarified in their mutual interaction.[2]

If the formality of God appeared to Jesus in his always being greater, the content of this reality is that he is love and *partial love.* Jesus found the prime setting for discernment in his radical openness to this greater God; this setting is love of man, and in this sense the *greater* God appears as the *lesser* God. While the sovereign will of God would seem on principle to admit all natural and historical mediations, the setting for discernment became particularized for Jesus in love of his neighbour. The classic passages in which Jesus's discerning consciousness are embodied: the Sabbath is made for man; his commandment of love for one's neighbour; no man has greater love than he who lays down his life for his friend: all have to be read from this theological and not merely ethical perspective. This provides a surprising 'making himself lesser' by God; a surprisingly lessened mediation of the primary will of God through love of one's neighbour.[3]

This appearance of the will of God in small things becomes even clearer to Jesus when the mediation of love appears partial and consciously partialized. The first setting for acting in accordance with the will of God is the service of love to the poor, the little, the oppressed. These are the privileged face of God in history and these are those who understand the kingdom. This is why they are, without doubt, the primary and irreplaceable setting for finding the will of God.

These simple observations—which obviously need development in all their complexity—claim to show that for Jesus the problem of the first and basic discernment was nothing other than the quest for the very reality of God and the place where this quest could meet God. Jesus' particular discernments then came, at least logically, after this one great discernment, although historically this first discernment went on developing through all the particular choices he made. This observation seems to me important if we are not to make the discernof Jesus and our own discernment a matter of regional theology, of mere spiritual theology or religious psychology; since however simple it seems, what we have said underlies all Christian discernment; the genuineness of particular discernments will arise from the conviction, not from routine repetition of the fact, that God is greater and partial love.

So the original experience that Jesus had of God, his Father, has to be taken in complete seriousness. This experience has recently been summarized as: 'God is always greater (and, if one likes, is by virtue of this fact also lesser) than culture, science, the Church, the Pope and everything institutional' (K. Rahner); and: 'the question is not whether someone is looking for God or not, but whether he is looking for him where he himself said he was' (P. Miranda).

THE DISCERNMENT OF JESUS AS A PROTOTYPE
OF THE STRUCTURE OF EVERY CHRISTIAN DISCERNMENT

Before analyzing the structure of the discernment of Jesus, I would like to make two preliminary observations. The first is that the title of this section is properly a statement of christological faith. Accepting that the discernment of Jesus provides the *prototype* of every Christian discernment, is a reformulation of christological orthodoxy that cannot be analyzed further. It is another way of stating the finalness of Jesus as the believer by definition, 'he who has lived the faith in fullness and from the beginning' (Heb. 12:2), in whom the basic way of corresponding to the Father is revealed. The second is that I am concentrating on the *structure* of the discernment of Jesus, which is what we should in fact pursue, while the particular solutions to our discernments cannot and should not be identical to those of Jesus. From Jesus we learn not so much the replies to our discernments as, more basically, how to learn to discern. We learn this not so much by analyzing the internal psychology of Jesus in his process of discernment, but on the basis of the choices and historical commitments that Jesus made. This *effected* discernment of Jesus supposes a channel of discernment which is the one we should pursue ourselves.

If we turn now to analyzing the particular structure of Jesus' discernment, we can say that along with his first appreciation of a God who is partial love for the poor, Jesus saw the love of God unconditionally placed between a 'yes' and a 'no'. The unconditional 'no' was directed at sin against the kingdom of God: that is against everything that dehumanizes man, that brings him death as man, that threatens, impedes, or annuls the human brotherhood expressed in the *Our Father*. However difficult it may seem to discern what has to be done in particular situations, there was at least a clear criterion of discernment for Jesus. 'The will of God is not a mystery, at least in so far as it applies to the brother and concerns love'.[4] The first step toward discernment is therefore hearing the clear 'no' given by God to the world of sin that dehumanizes man and has nothing mysterious about it, and above all, *carrying on* this 'no' throughout history without trying to stifle or soften this voice in any way whatsoever, not even—as is frequently done—with apparently orthodox theodicies. The second corresponding step is hearing God's 'yes' to a world that has to be reconciled, and above all, *carrying on* the Utopia of this 'yes' as a task never to be abandoned even when history so often questions it in a radical way. We will therefore be exercising discernment as long as we maintain this consciousness alive and do not give way to the scepticisms, realisms and even cynicisms that history offers us as more sensible solutions; we will exercise discernment by remaining radically open to the praxis of love and the overcoming of sin objectivized in history. It is therefore not so much a question of purifying our *intention* with regard to love, nor of reconciling the sinner in his *innerness*. Even though this is also necessary, Jesus' discernment was directed primarily to corresponding to the objectivity *in* history of God's 'yes' and 'no' *to* history.

The history of Jesus provides us *a posteriori* with criteria for a praxis of love that discerns which praxis and criteria should become for us the channel along which we should discern in our turn. The first criterion is *partial incarnation* in history.

For Jesus becoming incarnate did not mean setting himself in the totality of history so as to correspond to the totality of God from there; it meant rather choosing that particular spot in history that was capable of leading him to the totality of God. This spot is none other than the poor and the oppressed. Conscious of this partiality, which reached him as an alternative to other partialities based on power, or to an innocuous universalism which always means collaboration with power, Jesus from the beginning understood his mission as one destined to the poor; he unfolded his incarnation historically in solidarity with the poor and in the parable of the final judgment, declared the poor and the oppressed to be the setting from which the praxis of love can be discerned.

The second criterion is an *effective praxis* of love. Jesus sought the will of God by seeking particular and effective solutions. Jesus sought not only to announce a good news but to bring it about. He sought to convert the *good news* into a *good reality*. The whole of his public life, his miracles, his forgiveness, his controversies, bear witness to this, and an important part of the effectiveness he sought consisted in giving particular historical names to what constitutes sin and what constitutes love. Although Jesus obviously lacked modern techniques of analysis deriving from the social sciences, the Gospels show his definite tendency to call things by their name. His giving particular names to the sin of the rich, the powerful, the priests and the governors; his telling, for example, the rich young man what he had to do, are—although in rudimentary form—expressions of the need for particular mediations if love is to be historically effective and a transforming force.

The third criterion is a *praxis of socio-political love,* that is a love that becomes justice. Although love is extended on principle to any type of relationships created between persons (on the matrimonial, family, friendship, professional level, and so on) the history of Jesus bears clear witness to the fact that the efficacy of love must be applied to the configuration of the whole of society; and the Gospels, furthermore, show that in fact and historically, Jesus gave this type of love the first place in his own praxis. The basic reason for this is that the God of Jesus is the God of the kingdom who seeks to re-create the whole man and all men, and the form of love that we call justice corresponds to this type of social totality. The other forms of love applying to other areas of human life, will be kept up and will take on new forms from the basis of the justice of the Kingdom of God.

The fourth criterion is openness to a *conflictive love,* precisely because this love has to be partial, effective and socio-political. Conflictivity is intrinsic to the love of Jesus from the moment when he conceived his universality, from the particular standpoint of the oppressed. While the love of Jesus is *for* all men, its particular embodiment was seen by him to be in the first instance *with* the oppressed and *against* the oppressors precisely in order to humanize them all, to make them all brothers in history and in fact. This intrinsically conflicting nature also explains the extrinsic conflict that overtook the practice of Jesus' love in the form of polemic, rejection, persecution and death, as all the Gospels witness. The *gratuitous* dimension of Jesus' love is also shown historically in this way, a dimension not opposed to efficacy, but one that arises when the power of the world tilts against an effective love and this holds firm even though its efficacy cannot be clearly felt.

This specific praxis of love with these characteristics shows the discernment practiced by Jesus in his quest for the will of a God who is partialized love, and *through* this praxis we can also glimpse some formal characteristics of this discernment that converge with the reality of the greater God.

From this formal point of view, the first thing to say is that Jesus did not only discern at a given moment, nor were his momentary judgments the most important, but that his discernment had a *historical development*. The fact that God is greater did not come to Jesus from momentary consideration of his transcendence, but through the process and praxis of his love. This is why his life not only went through different chronological stages but also through different theological stages; and why we should speak of a 'conversion' of Jesus, since he did not absolutize or validate forever the particular form of building the kingdom and responding to the Father that he saw in the first stage of his life. This historicity of Jesus' discernment also includes its openness to risk, to making a choice in darkness, since he knew that it was more dangerous to interrupt this very process of discernment than to risk falling into error.

In the second place, the formality of Jesus' discernment was responsible for presenting his quest for the will of God in a *radical* form precisely because God is greater. One way in which this radicality appeared clearly in Jesus' manner of presenting discernment in the form of alternatives rather than as complementary: one cannot serve two masters, one cannot serve both God and mammon, one cannot guide the plough and look behind, one cannot win life and keep it. By presenting the formal structure of discernment in this way, Jesus deprived it of ingenuousness. Discernment is the exercise not of ingenuous goodwill but of a critical will, one that explicitly takes account of possible alibis even when they are disguised as good in order to achieve what really has to be done. Jesus exercised discernment when faced with alternatives presented as supposedly neuter, or even good: as power, riches and honour could appear to be. The radical nature of his discernment appears in his unmasking of his other possible options, which he shows not to be complementary but detrimental to the true reality of God.

The final characteristic of the form taken by Jesus's discernment is its *openness to verification*. One must therefore progress, from a good clear conscience before discerning, to a good objective conscience after having discerned. Jesus's own history and his statements on true following of him offer some criteria for verifying if this is the case: if discernment ends with a true praxis of the kingdom and not mere orthodox declarations; if this praxis has been produced through sacrifice; if this praxis results in the poor and the oppressed 'hearing' the kingdom; if the power of sin has felt truly threatened and has reacted by way of rejection and persecution; if the man who discerns models himself on the ideal of the Sermon on the Mount; if the historical and conflictive struggle to instal the kingdom makes Christians pass from their first generic faith, hope and charity to a faith proof against incredulity, hope proof against hope and justice proof against oppression. The importance of these observations for the process of discernment is that through objective verification, the setting of discernment is transposed from pure intention to historical objectivity, and that these objective criteria prepare the discerning subject better for successive discernments. The terrifying lucidity of the final 'may thy will be done' of Jesus' prayer in the garden was really prepared by the objective verifications of earlier discernments.

DISCERNMENT IN THE SPIRIT OF JESUS

Since his resurrection Jesus has been present through his Spirit but physically absent; the first Christians began to build the kingdom of God but this has not yet reached its fullness; the channel for following Jesus has been definitively approved by the Father, but the Spirit forces us to continue discerning in history. This produces an objective difficulty in continuing to speak of discernment. The formal solution is clear: 'discernment is required to recognize the actions in which this Spirit should show itself and strengthen itself, but not the basic way of life',[5] but Christology makes it difficult to see what the actual content of this discernment is to be. Christology, like Jesus, becomes modest; it offers a way of discernment but not a new law. The first-born gives way to his brothers for them to carry on building history according to the ideal of the kingdom of God. Therefore, and on principle, one cannot speak *a priori* and in the abstract of what discernment should be today, since this would be setting limits to the Spirit and denying the greater being of God for our own history. So, to end this study I would rather produce some meaningful examples of discernment brought about in the Church in Latin America. Examples that show the novelty of the Spirit moving—as I believe and hope—within the channel that Jesus showed us.

The first discernment, parallel to Jesus' case, is that of the real divinity of God. Faced with a history that shows us a God basically provident in history and eschatological beyond history, we find the truth of this God when he hears the clamour of the oppressed, demands justice and announces liberation, leaving the ultimate fullness of history to his loving mystery. The achievement of this discernment has come about in distinction and opposition to the idea of God handed on by so-called Western civilization and the culture of Christendom. It has been produced by denying the reality of a God of power, a God who historically has shown himself as an oppressor, either subtly, as has often happened through religious and ecclesiastical traditions, or crudely in the image of the divinity hidden in the ruling systems, whether they call themselves Capitalism, National Security, Multinationals or Trilateralism. I believe that this discernment has been achieved by the Spirit placing Christians not at the power centre but on the periphery of poverty.

This brings me to the basic discernment that I see as having been achieved in Latin America: today the Spirit is breathing strongly in the midst of an oppressed people. In their particular tribulations and desires, we see what the Spirit of Jesus wants here and now, what must undoubtedly be done and what particular sin must be removed, even if it seems as small and particular as that hope expressed in the Old Testament: 'they will build houses and live in them, they will plant vines and eat their fruit, they will not build for others to live, they will not plant for others to eat' (Is. 65:21). This Spirit of Jesus and the will of God appear through these hopes and fears however apparently disproportionately small they may be in comparison with the reality of a greater God.

In meeting the Spirit in the poor today, the Church is also beginning to become a Church of the poor,[6] thereby putting into practice—that is discerning—what Vatican II stated truly but generically on the subject of the Church as the people of God. It will be a Church in which everyone supports each other, but in this support, the poor have the privileged function of converting the others, of helping them to their faith.

And as the Church of the poor, it is the sacrament of liberation; it is not the reality of the kingdom of God but is at the service of this kingdom; but again, it will be the poor who will be responsible for making this generic truth—which can be automatically repeated from other points of view—produce, that is discern, particular consequences. The Church does not monopolize the service of the kingdom of God but welcomes all men of good will in this task and seeks to collaborate with them; it allows the various charisms—even of those who are outside it; it judges between true and false prophets not according to *a priori,* ecclesial criteria, but according to whether or not they are building the kingdom for the poor.[7] The Church has discerned that the important thing is for the kingdom to become reality, not for it to monopolize the understanding and the praxis of this kingdom, even though it will always offer everyone the channel Jesus provided to bring it about in truth.

The meaning of Christian love for the poor has also been discerned, charity has its own history; it has been assistential, promotional, and is now seen to be structural. This is a discernment of maximum importance, not because it outdates the other forms of charity, but because the Spirit has forced the poor to appreciate that this is the case. From this it also follows that charity is discerned as having to be a political love if it is to be effective, and that the secular mediations of the social, economic and political structures that most clearly serve the poor have also been discerned.[8]

These discernments, which I see as having been brought about recently in Latin America, obviously go beyond the particular contents of the discernment of Jesus, but they have been effected—I believe— through following the channel Jesus provided. This is why they are self-evidently right even though they remain subject to the criteria of verification I have set out and open to the final eschatological reserve. Here we come to the root of the need expressed at the beginning of this article to set Christian discernment within the trinitarian reality of God. As Christians we discern within the channel of following Jesus, with particular values, criteria and verifications. Within this channel, we listen to the requirements of the Spirit given to us to enable us to go on making history, following Jesus, and to go on initiating the kingdom of God in particular situations. The final verification of whether we are doing this consists in whether the Father continues to appear as the greater God and as that reality which is effective and partial love for the poor of the earth. When the day comes when it is no longer necessary to discern in this way, the kingdom of God will have arrived and he will be all in all.

Translated by Paul Burns

Notes

1. Many of the points in this article are dealt with at greater length in my book *Cristología desde América Latina* (Mexico, [2]1977), pp. 67–151.

2. It should be said in passing that Jesus' ignorance, on the theological level, is the condition of his discernment: knowledge of a greater God is only possible from the standpoint of not knowing. Of course, I am dealing throughout the article with the relationship between Jesus as creature and his Father, not the intra-trinitarian relationship between the Son and the Father.

3. For this 'belittling' of God, v. *Cristología desde América Latina*, pp. 141–49.

4. E. Käseman, *La llamada a la Libertad* (Salamanca, 1975), p. 35.

5. I. Ellacuría, 'La Iglesia que nace del pueblo por el Espíritu', in *Misión Abierta* 71 (1978), pp. 155ff.

6. Idem, 'La Iglesia de los pobres, sacramento histórico de liberación', in *Estudios Centroamericanos* 348/9 (1977), pp. 707–22.

7. Cf. E. Dussel, 'Differentiation of Charisms', in *Concilium* 129 (1977).

8. This is the standpoint for understanding the extensive and weighty discussions on the relationship between the Church and capitalism or socialism as a process of discernment of how to *bring about* the kingdom of God in practice. Cf. J. L. Segundo, 'Capitalism-Socialism: the Theological Crux', in *Concilium* 96 (1974); I. Ellacuría, 'Economic Theories and the Relationship between Christianity and Socialism', in *Concilium* 125 (1977).

PART II

History

W. A. M. Peters

Ignatius of Loyola and 'Discernment of Spirits'

FAIRLY generally, Ignatius is considered to be one of the greatest masters in the art of discerning spirits, perhaps now more so than ever, witness the spate of articles, the numerous seminars and workshops devoted to this matter.[1] As a rule such great interest does not so much point to a deeply felt need, as to many unexpected difficulties in bringing clarity; for, if the answer to questions had been found, there would be less groping for solutions to problems that present themselves, and there can be little doubt that there is room for correction. Indeed, the very opening statement of this essay is open to criticism. First, there is the choice of the word *art*. Ignatius was well aware that true discernment is a charism, a gift from God, and as such an action on the part of man soaked in prayer. So much is abundantly clear from the text of the Spiritual Exercises, but also from the famous, even notorious example in Ignatius' own life, the so called 'deliberatto primorum patrum', when Ignatius and his first companions in 1539 tried to find out whether God wanted them to continue as they were, a loose gathering of priests engaged in various forms of apostolate, or to achieve a greater unity and stability by becoming a religious community. The advantages and disadvantages of the two alternatives were carefully examined and weighed, but all this with much prayer before and during and after by a group of exceptionally spiritual men. One conclusion stands out: if 'discernment of spirits' is a charism (cf. I Cor. 12:10; 1 Jn. 4:1), one should be very cautious about methods, techniques, and so on.

Second, a serious objection to our opening statement concerns the very expression *discernment of spirits*. Ignatius does not really discern spirits. The well known rules (Sp. Ex. 313–336) [2] are introduced by: 'reglas para en alguna manera sentir y congnoscer las varias mociones que en la anima se causan' (313). The use of the passive voice ('se causan') should be noticed (cf. 316) as well as the absence of any reference to spirits. Ignatius now immediately mentions all sorts of movements that in varied circumstances are caused in different persons (314–317). If there are no 'mociones' or 'agitaciones' (317, 6), the retreatant should be asked some questions, for Ignatius now ponders what is amiss. Again, Ignatius does not want the retreatant to reveal his own thoughts and sins, but he does want to know about the 'agitaciones' and thoughts that come from different spirits (17). Although Ignatius does use the expression *discernment of spirits* (176, 328), to anyone who is familiar with the text and the contents of the Spiritual Exercises it must be evident that he is really occupied with all sorts of movements: the *being* enlightened, the *being* moved and stirred, the *being* assailed and tempted, etc. Throughout the exercises from the very beginning it is not spirits that play the main part, but movements, and the reason or cause is that from the first beginnings the implications of annotation 5, 15, 16 and 20, just to mention a few, are never realized without a dire struggle, without the retreatant being tossed around a good deal, even unto the experience of being pulled apart. As the retreat proceeds, the situation does not improve from this point of view: in the fourth week 'mayores mociones y gustos spirituales' are to be expected (227), and throughout the retreat all these movements should be carefully examined ('bien examinados', 336). We find great difficulty in accepting a preoccupation with spirits, where evidently Ignatius is occupied with creating order, and consequently with doing away all 'affecciones desordenadas' (cf. the title of the Sp. Ex.; 21, 1, 16), which surely are movements.[3]

Be it also noted that the verb *discernir* is never used, except once, and then its object is the proper time for making a sound election (336). The verbs preferred by Ignatius are *sentir, cognoscer*.[4]

These textual remarks lead to two important observations:

1. The object of discernment is, neither in the writings of Ignatius nor in his own life, the will of God (or, for that matter, true doctrine, genuine experience in prayer, real prophecy, and a host of other subjects mentioned by various authors). The emphasis on the will of God as the proper and primary object of discernment probably finds its origin in a certain predilection for the first method in the so-called third time of Ignatius to make a good election (179; see below). However,

with reference to the will of God Ignatius consistently uses the verbs *buscar* and *hallar,* often in combination (to seek, to find: cf. first and fifteenth annotations), while the normal ending of his letters contains the combination *sentir y cumplir.* We do well to be fully aware that discerning movements and seeking and finding the will of God have very little in common, except that, once movements have been properly discerned and hence clarified as to their whence, whereto and contents, darkness and confusion have been removed, and thus the retreatant will find himself in a much more favourable position to discover what pleaseth the Father.

2. As regards Ignatius' own life: not merely during the months of inactivity and forced reflection when he was recovering from his wounds, but also after his conversion when he was on his way to the Holy Land—and in this period falls his ten months stay at Manresa—and throughout his life, he was assailed by all sorts of movements, ranging from contemplated suicide to intense joy at a vision of the Trinity. These extremes span a rich diversity of movements: some emotional and psychological, some profoundly spiritual, some coming from God, others from the 'enemy of human nature' (135, 325–327, 334; 7, 8, 10), all of them either directly or indirectly. Ignatius wanted clarity in this medley of varied movements. Once insight and clarity is gained, that is, once they have been properly discerned, some will be rejected ('lanzar') as dangerous, worthless, coming from the evil spirit, others will be accepted ('recibir') and cherished (cf. 313). That is all. In the end it is a question of being moved by God or of not being moved by God, but such a movement of God is gift and value by itself, totally irrespective of whether it is geared to finding the will of God in a certain situation. Naturally, when Ignatius speaks of accepting a certain movement, the will of God is involved in as far as God wants him to accept his movement, but the movement itself need not at all be linked with God's will in a specific case.

It is a point that needs to be stressed because unnecessary confusion is being caused by not accurately reading the text of the Spiritual Exercises or properly assessing Ignatius' own practice. Nowhere is this nowadays better illustrated than by the handling of what we referred to above, the first method of the third time of making a sound election (177–183). Briefly, the method comes to this, that the devout person, trying to find the will of God, weighs the advantages and disadvantages of two alternatives; the decision is then based upon the outcome of this procedure. The method is often considered to be most typically Ignatian, and it has gained great popularity, especially where communal discernment is practiced. We point out that the method is a way of finding the will of God, and has nothing to do with discerning movements. Further, it is strictly limited to the area of a mutable choice ('election mutable' 179); where there is question of an immutable choice, Ignatius will have none of it. Moreover, Ignatius did not have much confidence in this method. When the task has been performed, he demands that the person should pray hard ('ir con mucha diligencia a la oración' 183) really to find out whether his own investigations tally with God's vision and judgment, which strongly suggests that he wants the person to move into the second time 'when a great deal of clarity and knowledge is gained through the experience of desolation and consolation and through the experience of discerning various spirits' (176). This sudden turn at the end is not surprising, for weighing the advantages and disadvantages in any mutable choice unavoidably involves the great gift of discerning movements, because any opinion, judgment, vision of any advantage or disadvantage is strongly influenced by 'affecciones', by inclinations (16, 179–181), even if one is not consciously aware of them.

It is not merely the confusion between discerning movements and discerning, i.e., seeking and finding, the will of God that has harmed a true understanding of Ignatian discernment. There occur to us three what we might call key words that have become closely associated with discernment, but in a somewhat irresponsible, and at times indefensible way: Ignatian discernment became too closely linked with the *election* to be made during the Spiritual Exercises; it became the indispensable accompaniment of *indifference,* and it became to a large extent identified with a certain number of *rules,* to be found in the text of the Exercises (313–336). As regards *election* as the goal of the Spiritual Exercises, the debate has not been laid to rest. There are still many who cannot but see the election of a state of life as the primary purpose of the Exercises. Now, there can be no doubt that in the Exercises an election always takes place as any decision implies a choice between alternatives, but we now use the word *election* almost in an analogical sense, its object no longer being a state of life, but something with a far wider connotation. This wider connotation is expressed in the title and the first annotation of the Exercises, namely 'to order one's life' and thus to bring all its details into harmony with God's will.[5] Unavoidably, connecting 'discerning spirits' (not: movements) with 'election' as the goal of the Exercises (which it is not) is asking for trouble and confusion.

As regards *indifference,* it came through a rather tenacious tradition to stand for a certain static immobility, the steady unmoved pointer of a pair of scales. This Ignatian illustration (15) has been used to clarify what indifference is supposed to mean. One is no longer moved one way or the other and one had to strive after this. Unfortunately, this illustration is not used at all with reference to the retreatant; it applies to the retreat master, who is told not to do any pushing. This interpretation of what indifference is appears very difficult to harmonize with the sixth annotation where Ignatius is suspicious of this sort of immobility or immovability; indifference as the absence of 'mociones y agitationes' might easily turn into a waiting attitude and thus clash with the fifth annotation in which the retreatant is asked not to wait, but to surrender, taking plenty of risks, offering His Creator and Lord his whole will and liberty, in order that his Divine Majesty might dispose of his person and all he has according to His most Holy Will. Indifference never stands for absence or repression of movements. On the contrary: the concern of both retreatant and retreat master is to see to it that the retreatant is not moved *too much* one way or the other, until he finds out where the movement or pull comes from (23, 16, 153–155, 157). It is then that, as a matter of right order, *lanzar* and *recibir* play their part.

As regards the *rules* given by Ignatius and their relationship with discerning movements (and we point out once again that the verbs used by Ignatius in this context are *sentir* and *cognoscer*: 313), some of them are more applicable to the first week, the second set more to the second week (313, 9; 328, 10). Certain obvious questions present themselves at once. What about rules for the third week, for the fourth week? The answer appears to be that on the one hand the movements will be of the same kind, only more intense and profound (Ignatius refers to 'mayores mociones y gustos spirituales' 227), that on the other the retreatant will have learnt how to discern, and need little more help than Ignatius could give. Another question is why Ignatius added 'to a certain extent', 'in a certain way' ('en alguna manera', 313). Does this modestly suggest that Ignatius does not consider himself at all the grand master of discerning movements? that he is not too certain himself of the value of his rules? that he is so much aware that true discernment is God's gift and God's work that he does not go beyond pointing out some easily observable facts and easily made mistakes, beyond directing attention to indispensable conditions and ever-present obstacles? Now, an objective reading of the rules takes any doubt away that Ignatius is doing exactly that. All the rules taken together do not make up a method or technique for discerning movements; they still leave us pretty helpless, except in as far as we are warned about what might easily happen, of what mistakes are too quickly made, about what matters of importance are lightly overlooked. The rules mostly set the stage for a proper discernment of movements, laying down conditions, trying to remove obstacles. Thereafter no method is available: it is by standing in the light that it can be discerned whence movements come, whereto they move. Thus Ignatius points out that spiritual maturity is a factor of importance (314–315; 9–10), that ways and means frequently used by Satan have to be taken into account, and especially that he works in terms of peace, light, comfort, persuasiveness, reasonableness, etc., as befits him as 'an angel of light' (331), that God can and does interfere directly (330), that a movement is not momentaneous, like a flash, but often a process, with a beginning, a middle and an ending, spread over days or even weeks (333). This appears very difficult to reconcile with the practice of cutting a movement into pieces of a day's duration: the mistake that underlies a growing practice of having a retreatant give a *detailed* account of what happened to him or her in the course of the day and the day's exercises. It appears also to be irreconcilable with counselling on a from-day-to-day basis, as neither the retreatant nor, and even less, the retreat master is able each evening properly and accurately to discern what God is doing, which way he is moving, where Satan is at work, where man's wounded nature is reacting, etc.

'En alguna manera' stands above all for caution, or if it is preferred, discretion, which should evolve towards Ignatius' *discreta caritas,* a key expression in his Constitutions. Peace is not just peace, and joy is not just joy, and desolation is not just desolation. That is precisely where discernment comes in. We have too often seen peace taken to be a movement from and towards God, while in actual fact it was no more than the result of a conflict ended; we have seen joy taken to be the fruit of the Spirit, while actually the movement was nothing but Satan moving man into false security, or even the result of a good meal. Desolation was taken to be a movement through which Satan alienates man from God, while in fact the movement was an excess of consolation, of God overwhelming the poor soul with an unmanagable abundance of his peace and love. Although such instances might be called classical, it is sadly surprising how people still rush in where angels fear to tread ('en alguna manera'!) and where prudent discernment has to yield to hasty conclusions.

It would not be fair if, with the many and very diverse movements in the life of the Church before us, we were to keep separate discernment of movements and the interest taken in, and the value attached to, *spontaneity,* at times closely associated with the charismatic renewal movement. Spontaneity is quickly taken to be identical with being moved by the Spirit, to be some sort of release of the Spirit: *quod demonstrandum est.* Surely, the history of the Church is there to prove that more often than not spontaneity stands for superficiality; what floats on the top of our consciousness forces its way out, wants to express itself; but this is no guarantee whatever that such spontaneous movement is inspired and guided by God's Spirit. If anywhere, it is in this area of spontaneity that Ignatius' warning of careful examination ('bien examinados' 336) should be taken to heart. This is the reason why on the whole the Spiritual Exercises are low-keyed; even at the end there is not any exuberant enthusiasm: the retreatant is advised to turn to God in deep humility and pray: 'take and receive', which is followed by 'but give me your grace and love', notice as gifts.

There is no mistaking a certain hesitant wisdom in Ignatius' handling of the whole matter of discerning movements. Such caution was not merely born of his own experience. He had seen in his dealings with other persons and painfully observed in what was happening in the Church how even saintly men were led astray with most painful and disastrous results. We here refer to the Inquisitors, often men moved by love for the Church, inspired by a burning desire to see doctrine kept pure and undefiled, who had no doubt that these movements originated with God . . . we now know better and see more clearly. Ignatius knew that at a time when Christians were exposed to a greater diversity of very impressive movements under the influence of the Renaissance and the (Counter-) Reformation, discernment was not made easier but more imperative.

Wisdom, caution, prudence, prayer lie at the root of Ignatian discernment of the many movements man is exposed to. These are caused by spirits, but also by the Spirit, which implies that they are not all and all the time subject matter of psychological analysis or counselling. Such methods may help a little, but in the end it is the experience of consolation and desolation (176) together with the openness and surrender of the fifth, fifteenth and twentieth annotations that will greatly contribute to the clarity we long for and need badly.

Notes

1. A useful, though by no means complete or entirely satisfactory, survey is given in *The Discernment of Spirits*, a study by G. D. Coleman (Jersey City, 1973).

2. When referring to the text of the Spiritual Exercises, I use the Marietti edition of 1928 and I adopt the marginal numbers there introduced and now generally accepted.

3. H. Coathalem, S.J., identifies for all practical purposes movement and spirit: 'spirit, virtually equivalent of movement'. *Ignatian Insights* (Taichling, Taiwan, 1961), p. 245.

4. A scholarly useful study of Ignatian terminology is given by J. C. Futrell, S.J., in his *Making an Apostolic Community of Love* (St Louis, 1970), pp. 106–19. Cf. also 'Ignatian Discernment' in *Studies in the Spirituality of Jesuits*, II (April, 1970), pp. 47–88, by the same author.

5. Cf. W. A. M. Peters, S.J., *The Spiritual Exercises of St. Ignatius: Exposition and Interpretation* (Jersey City, 1967), pp. 5–8.

Jose M. Castillo

The Imitation of Christ and *The Way:*
a Matter of Discernment

THE *Imitation of Christ,* whose author appears to have been Thomas à Kempis [1] has, after the Bible, been the most widely read book of the last five centuries. There are 700 manuscripts in existence and 89 incunabula. Since its first edition in 1470, it has been translated into 95 languages and by now has run into more than 3,000 editions. [2]

The Way is the most important work by Mgr Escrivá de Balaguer, the founder of Opus Dei. It was first published in 1934 under the title of 'Spiritual Considerations'. The author put it into its final form during the Spanish Civil War, in Burgos which was then the capital of that part of Spain under the control of General Franco. By April 1977 it had run into 138 editions in 34 languages and sold a total of more than 2.5 million copies. [3]

The Imitation of Christ and *The Way* are two very different books, different in their origin, their quality and their content, but both have one thing in common: they are both writings that have had an important influence on Christian people. From this point of view, they can be considered two 'typical' works. Consequently they can be seen as two paradigms of spirituality, extremely useful for appreciating the rôle that Christian discernment has played in the lives of many Christians.

DISCERNMENT AND THE CHRISTIAN SPIRIT

Discernment is not a secondary matter in the sum total of the Christian life. On the contrary, the New Testament shows discernment as the criterion for giving us the measure of the Christian spirit. By this I mean: the authentically Christian spirit contained in a particular programme of spirituality is defined by what this programme tells us about discernment. Consequently if a book which claims to be a programme for the spiritual life tells us nothing about Christian discernment, we can say with absolute certainty that this book has only a superficial coat of varnish of the spirit of the Gospel, and we can even state that this book in its basic inspiration is not Christian.

In fact, discernment is the expression of the genuine worship of Christians (Rom. 12, 1–2), the putting into practice of their journey through life as 'sons of the light' in contradistinction to the 'sons of darkness' (Eph. 5:10), the mechanism which, through love, can lead them to discover what the will of God is (Phil. 1:9–10), the solution when faced with deceit and when faced with the possible deviations we can suffer on our Christian journey (1 Jn. 4:1; cf. Phil. 1:10–11), the overall realization of our maturity in the Christian life (Heb. 5:14). The believer, therefore, finds what God wants in a particular situation and circumstance by means of Christian discernment.[4]

This discernment does not consist in applying the law to particular cases, nor does it consist in unconditionally submitting one's own conscience to the dictates of someone else, the spiritual director. The New Testament says nothing to suggest this. Discernment consists in a strictly personal experience, the experience of Christian love. This love, which invades the affective life of the believer, is the mainspring of a sensitivity and a penetrating knowledge in man (Phil. 1:9–10) which enable him to discover with a certain naturalness and spontaneity what it is that pleases the Lord.

This discovery is made by virtue of certain values. The scale of values opposed to the 'world', that is the 'present order' and the system established on the basis of 'the strong' (1 Cor. 1:28), prestige and influence, power and domination.[5] The will of God can only be discovered from the 'new mind' (Rom. 12:2); that is, from the scale of values that places 'the weak', the poor and despised, the plebeian and what does not count (1 Cor. 1:26–9) above everything else, contrary to the 'masters of our age', who crucified the Lord (1 Cor. 2:6–8).[6]

A spirituality is Christian to the extent and only to the extent—that it makes man capable of discovering for himself, through the means of discernment, what the will of God is. And furthermore, it must do this on the basis of a 'new mind' which is not the mentality of effectiveness, nor even the mentality of the apostolate, but the disconcerting mentality of those who 'follow' Jesus in service to the weak, the poor and the despised—even to the cross.

THE 'IMITATION OF CHRIST': PRIVATIZED DISCERNMENT

The term 'discernment' appears only once in the *Imitation of Christ*,[7] but as is well-known, the subject of discernment itself is in fact one of the main themes of the book.[8] Chapter 54 of the third book is devoted to it, but it is not dealt with in this chapter alone. One might say that the whole work—particularly this third book—is nothing other than a process of personal interiorization enabling the believer to discover for himself what it is that is pleasing to the Lord.

In this sense the constant recourse to one's own conscience [9] is eloquent, as is the invitation to discover for oneself what is the will of God [10] and to listen to his voice in one's heart, as opposed to those who allow themselves to be influenced by human words.[11] The same is true of the insistence on everything that helps to fill the affections [12] with fervour, and everything that produces true, inner freedom.[13]

This insistence on the inner life is what leads the author of *The Imitation* to despise external practices and to criticize pilgrimages and the cult of relics.[14] As has been truly said, this criticism of the externals characteristic of the piety of the Late Middle Ages and this insistence on inner justice, place the author of *The Imitation* as much in the line of the Protestant Reformation of the sixteenth century as of the Catholic reform.[15]

But in this matter of discernment, it is not sufficient for an author to recommend it enthusiastically. More important than this is the sum total of criteria the author provides for the reader, so that he can orient himself properly when seeking what God requires of him. Now this is where *The Imitation* not only stops half way but, worse than that, takes a line that one might today describe as 'way off'. In fact, the ethics of *The Imitation* show a broad predominance of contrast between the spiritual and the material, the invisible and the visible,[16] contempt for creation and the human in favour of supernatural grace.[17] This dualist mentality, imbued with philosophical currents alien to faith, has little that is Christian about it and is of course in no way in accord with the spirit or the letter of biblical revelation.

This, however, is still not the most important factor. Without any doubt, the most serious limitation of *The Imitation* lies in its unilateral insistence on the private sphere, the subjective and the individual. This is why it totally fails to broach such important questions for Christian life as community, the Apostolate and the very meaning of the Church.

Now this limitation cannot be resolved by finding an 'equilibrium' between private and public, subjective and objective, piety and liturgy, individual and community.[18] Setting things in this way gives the impression that what one is trying to achieve is an adequate cataloguing of these different elements or different dimensions in Christian existence, but there is a serious worry that this road will always leave us moving in inevitable ambiguity; and, what is worse, we will always be subject to a tension: the old tension between contemplation and action, between personal sanctification and the Apostolate, between the individual and the community.

The problem lies in seeing clearly, once and for all, whether Jesus' message is a message directed essentially to individuals (who then have to add the communitary dimension) or whether, on the contrary, the message is essentially directed to the community (within which individuals cannot evade their own personal responsibilities). In other words, the question lies in knowing whether the Christian event is essentially an individual and private event in which the public and communitary dimension then has to be integrated, or whether, on the contrary, the Christian event consists essentially in a communitary and public happening which then has to be lived from the standpoint of the necessary responsibility of each person. What should be said about this?

In the treatises of spiritual theology, it is said that the perfection of the Christian life consists essentially in love of God and love of one's neighbour.[19] Furthermore, the subject to which perfection is attributed is not the Christian life or the spiritual life, but the person. That is, the perfection of the Christian event consists, according to these masters of spirituality, in the perfecting of the individual.[20] Of course this individual is told that he has to love his neighbour, but the basic assumption made is that the essential pursuit of the Christian is *his own perfection*. In this way we find that the centre of Christian life is the *individual* not the *community:* that is, the centre is the *I* not the *We*. From this it follows that the Christian life is thought of as essentially ordered to individuals, not seen in relation to communities. *The Imitation of Christ* is fully in accordance with this mode of thought.

Now the New Testament shows that the message of Jesus is essentially communitary. Of course faith is man's personal response to God. From this point of view, faith is necessarily a matter for each individual, but this does not mean to say that faith should be an 'individual' affair; still less, that it should be a 'private' affair. Jesus' plan is essentially one for the community. Therefore Jesus' actions were always orientated toward the formation of the new people of God, the new community of salvation (Cf. Mt. 1:21; 2:6; Lk. 1:17, 68, 77; 2:10, 32;

3:15, 18; 17:16).[21] This is why Jesus from the outset of his public ministry devoted himself to gathering a group of people, the disciples, who formed his incipient community.[22] Furthermore, the life-project Jesus presented to this group was not a project of individual perfecting but an essentially communitary project. The Sermon on the Mount, which is the programme for the new community, has to be understood in this way. It is a community in which no division can be tolerated (Mt. 18; 15:17) nor differences of any kind since all are brothers (Mt. 23:9–11; Lk. 12:4; Jn. 15:15; Mt. 28:10; Jn. 20:17). This is how the early Church understood it from the beginning (Acts 2:44; 4:32). And this is how Paul taught it when he requested that all believers should be equal in the bosom of each community (2 Cor. 8:13–14; Gal. 3: 27–8; Cf. Col. 3:11; Rom. 14:7–9; 1 Cor. 3:21–3).

The Christian faith is an *essentially communitary project* in a particular sense: the believer is called not simply to 'do good' but above all, to 'make a community', sharing what he is and what he has with others in unconditional service to others, particularly to the poorest, the most unfortunate and the most persecuted. Put in another way, Jesus' project does not consist in a project of individual perfectioning, but in a programme for communities in which the present order is inverted and in which men set themselves to live in such a way that the 'present order' will be radically upset.

As a result one can say, undoubtedly, that the discernment presented by *The Imitation* is acceptable in its insistence on the desire to give oneself to Christ and on the inner freedom of the heart. But it is also a dangerous discernment because it leaves the community and public dimension of faith out of account. By leaving something so essential out of account, the generosity and enthusiasm it seeks to engender can result in the most dangerous alienation, because devotion, piety, mortification and all other spiritual practices can then act as tranquilizers to the conscience, to the point where the individual is incapable of understanding that Jesus came into the world not only that there should be *saints* but, above all, that there should be *communities* in the world. A faith that fails to understand this is an alienated faith.

'THE WAY': THE NEGATION OF DISCERNMENT

The Opus Dei, as is well known, has been a much debated institution over the last thirty years, admired by some and attacked by others. The one indisputable fact is that the Opus Dei has proved itself capable of forming its members in such a way as to make them fully devoted and unconditionally disciplined in their religious commitments and their Apostolate. This, it would appear, is the secret of the success that the Work of Mgr Escrivá has been reaping since its foundation.

The Way, the most important work of the 'Father' (as Mgr Escrivá is called in the Opus Dei), admirably describes the spirit and the mystique that inspire the members of this remarkable institution. This spirit and mystique lay abundant stress on love of Jesus Christ, on the need for an inner life, on generosity and commitment to the apostolate and on other virtues, such as purity, charity, humility and mortification. Mgr Escrivá is not original in all this; his spirituality is the spirituality of all times, as has always been taught, more or less, by writers on piety, devotion and the spiritual life.

But the spirit of the members of the Opus Dei has something else very special about it: an unconditional commitment admitting neither doubts nor suspicions, intolerant of the slightest criticism and binding all the men and women who belong to the 'Work' into a perfectly disciplined body. Recently, an authoress who has belonged to the Opus for many years and held important offices in it, wrote on this aspect:

> By the fact of belonging to the Work, one would always be on the right path, able to give sure teaching to those unfortunates whose beliefs are mistaken, distorted, ignorant and ingenuous; because as soon as one arrives, one is swallowed-up, supported and guaranteed by the directors, people specially chosen (as we must see), who, through being united to the Father, possess the gift of inerrancy because the Father is never mistaken and in the Work everything goes through the Father: 'you must pass everything through my head and through my heart', Mgr Escrivá has frequently told the directors.[23]

This is why the same writer goes on to state: 'the spiritual sufficiency experienced in the Work is most impressive, based as it is on this direct line, on this "hot line", uniting the Founder with God without intermediaries. "Heaven is determined that the Work will be carried out" through what Mgr Escrivá thinks and proposes. Therefore, there is nothing to fear. Neither is there *anything* to discuss with *anybody:* "God wishes it and that is enough". We only have to look upwards, freeing ourselves from all worries, leaving aside personal needs, including the need to reason.' [24]

One might be forgiven for thinking that this is an exaggerated reaction. It would seem almost impossible for there to be anyone so fanatical and therefore so curiously alienated. And yet, anyone who reads Mgr Escrivá's principal work carefully will come to see that the root of this fanaticism and alienation is right there in the book.

In fact, one of the things that strikes one most forcibly when reading

The Way is the spirit of self-sufficiency and superiority it engenders in anyone who identifies with its teachings. So, every member of the Opus Dei cannot be one of the 'heap': because 'he is born to be a leader' (no. 16).[25] So he has to 'soar like the eagles' (no. 7), he has to be 'guide, chief, leader!' to force, push and drag others along, not only through his example and his word, but also through his knowledge and his mastery (no. 19). He must have 'ambitions: to know, to lead, to be bold' (no. 24). He has to follow 'the way up with holy unconcern' (no. 44). This is because 'equality as it is generally understood is synonymous with injustice' (no. 46). Undoubtedly the 'Father' wants his children in the Opus to set themselves on a separate level, on a higher plane. This is why he orders them in no uncertain terms: 'if you feel the impulse to be a leader, let your aspiration be this: with your brothers the last; with the rest the first' (no. 365). This is why the members of the Opus must place themselves 'in the first rank as group leaders' (no. 411). As Mgr Escrivá is not satisfied with a little, his aspiration is to 'everything great' (no. 821), to 'impressive grandeur' (no. 823), to 'gigantic adventures' (no. 826). This is why his constant advice becomes understandable: 'leaders! . . . Your will must be made virile so that God will make you leaders' (no. 833).

This self-sufficiency, this ambition to greatness and this spirit of superiority are based on the peculiar way in which Mgr Escrivá conceives the manner in which one should be holy in the Opus Dei. *The Way*, in its no. 387, states: 'the level of sanctity which the Lord requires of us is determined by these three points: holy instransigence, holy coercion and holy effrontery'. These expressions, ingenuous or perhaps petulant as they may seem, are the most outright affirmation of someone who sees himself as possessing undebatable truth without the possibility of doubts or deviations. The 'Father' states that 'transigence is the sure sign of not possessing the truth' (no. 394). From this it follows that 'a transigent man will once more condemn Jesus to death' (no. 393).

How can one explain this degree of obstinacy and certainty of oneself? The reply is very simple. The first thing to notice about *The Way* is that it never mentions Christian discernment—to the extent that there is not a single allusion to it in the whole book. This means clearly that Mgr Escrivá ignores what has rightly been called the key to moral behaviour according to the New Testament.[26] It also means that *The Way* falls outside the spiritual tradition of the Church.[27] But above all it means that truth and good for members of the Opus Dei are not something for man to discover by himself, but something imposed on him, something to be accepted without question because all good and all truth are to be found in this acceptance.

This is not an exaggeration, nor is it a malicious interpretation. no. 377 of *The Way* has Mgr Escrivá telling the fervent follower of the Work: 'and how shall I acquire "our formation" and how shall I keep "our spirit"? By fulfilling the specific directions which your Director gave you and explained to you and made you love: carry these out and you will be an Apostle'. He is talking of a special formation—'our formation'—and of a special spirit—'our spirit'. This formation and spirit consist in carrying out for the 'Father'—that is for Mgr Escrivá (*carrying me out*)—the specific rules dictated by the Director. There is no recourse to the Gospel nor to Christian tradition. The formation and spirit are based on the norms dictated by the Director.

This means that obedience in the Opus Dei is a matter of life and death, of being or not being: 'obedience . . . the sure way, blindly obeying the superior . . . the way of holiness. Obedience in your apostolate . . . , the only way: because in God's work the spirit has to be obedient or take his leave' (no. 941). One has to be obedient even in 'ridiculous' details (no. 618) and in what appears 'sterile' (no. 623). Because, finally, 'it is the will of God that the Captain should steer the ship in order to lead us to a safe port through his light and knowledge' (no. 59). Direction, therefore, is not attributed to the Spirit but to a man, the Director, who is responsible for the building of 'the fortress of your sanctification' (no. 60).

Of course many masters of the spiritual life have recommended obedience, but these masters have insisted equally or even more on the need for discernment,[28] but not here. In the first place, because there is not a word about discernment. In the second, because *The Way* does not admit the slightest possibility of a spirit of criticism, of the right to think for oneself or question what one is commanded.[29]

Once one accepts this, everything becomes possible. The negation and alienation of the person become quite possible.[30] It is also possible for this person, on top of being alienated, to carry on with greater self-sufficiency and security,[31] and above all, it is possible to accept the unbridled use of money, power and prestige [32] as means of evangelization when in reality, these are the means the devil proposed to Jesus in the temptation in the desert.[33] The negation of discernment brings serious consequences in its train: the Gospel is perverted, faith alienated and the person destroyed.

CONCLUSION

The Imitation of Christ and *The Way* have been major influences on Christian people. After what we have said, this should make one think. In the first place, because *The Way* marks a regression when compared to *The Imitation,* since by negating Christian discernment it re-establishes the law and the rule as the necessary mediation between God and man. Secondly, because both *The Imitation* and *The Way* leave out of account whole aspects of the Gospel and thereby create real abysses between the believer and the Spirit of Jesus of Nazareth. *The Imitation* does this by leaving the essentially communitary dimension of faith out of account. *The Way* does it because it inevitably leads to alienation of the person and hardly disguised complicity with the 'world' that Jesus rejected and by which he was rejected even unto death.

This is why we have every right to state that discernment provides the measure of the authentically Christian spirit. Neither devotion nor generosity can be the decisive criterion of a life orientated toward the message of Jesus. The only criterion is the capacity of the man of faith to discern the ways of the Spirit.

Translated by Paul Burns

Notes

1. The present state of investigation into the question of authorship is very clearly set out in A. Ampe, 'Imitatio Christi. Le livre et l'auteur', in *Dict. de Spiritualité* VII/2, 2338–55.

2. Cf. E. Iserloh, 'Die Devotio moderna', in *Handbuch der Kirchengeschichte* III/2 (Freiburg, 1968), p. 535; A. de Backer, *Essai Biblioraphique sur le livre De Imitatio . . .* (Liège, 1864), pp. 221–45.

3. In English-speaking countries, *The Way* has had somewhat mixed fortunes, moving from one publisher and distributor to the next . . . Overall sales figures for the English editions are not available (Translator).

4. The most complete biblical study on discernment is G. Therrien, *Le discernement dans les écrits pauliniens* (Paris, 1973). I have analyzed the Pauline texts in my *El discernimiento cristiano según San Pablo* (Granada, 1975). Cf. also W. Grundmann, in *Theol. Wört. zum N. T.,* II, pp. 258–68.

5. In the terminology of the day, 'the world' (*kósmos*) expressed primarily order, particularly the juridical ordering of mankind. Cf. G. Haeffner, 'World', in *Sac. Mun.* 6 (London & New York, 1970). The equivalent in modern parlance would be 'the established order' or 'the system'. This 'order' is structured by a particular 'wisdom' (1 Cor. 1:20–25), that is by a scale of values implying valuing the wise and the strong 'in the ordinary sense of the word', and despising the weak and the common (1 Cor. 1:27–28); it belongs to the wise, the influential and the noble (1 Cor. 1:26).

6. In 1 Cor. 1:26, Paul lists three groups who form a minority in the commu-

nity: the wise, the influential and the noble. He chooses these to show how the wisdom of God differs from the wisdom of the world. So the 'world' is characterized by what these three groups of people usually have, what sets them apart: prestige, power and money. The 'new mind' of Romans 12:2 consists in not 'modelling yourselves on the behaviour of the world around you'.

7. He uses the verb *'discernere'*. III, 54. 1.

8. This is particularly noticeable in the third book. Cf. B. Spaapen, 'Imitatio Christi. Doctrine', in *Dict. de Spirit.* VII/2, 2365–66.

9. II, 2. 1; II, 4. 2; II, 6. 1; II, 6. 2; II, 6. 3; III, 23. 6; III, 43. 2; III, 48. 6; IV, 7. 1; IV, 11. 7.

10. I, 25. 2; III, 1. 1; III, 3. 6; III, 25. 3.

11. II, 1. 7; II, 6. 4; III, 1. 1; III, 2. 1, 2, 3.

12. III, 2. 3; III, 3. 5; III, 4. 2; III, 7. 1; III, 27. 1; III, 34. 1.

13. II, 8.5; III, 4. 2; III, 23. 1; III, 27, 1; III, 38. 1.

14. I, 11. 4; III, 58. 1, 2; IV, 1. 9.

15. Cf. E. Iserloh, op. cit., p. 537.

16. I, 22. 2, 4; I, 23. 1; II, 1. 4; II, 7. 1; II, 1. 1, 2; III, 11. 3; etc.

17. Especially chs. 54 and 55 of the third book.

18. Cf. F. Vandenbroucke, 'Why is the Imitation of Christ not read any more?', in *Concilium* 3. 7 (March, 1971).

19. Cf. O. Zimmermann, *Lehrbuch der Aszetik* (Freiburg, 1932), pp. 15 ff; J. de Guibert, *Theologia Spiritualis Ascetica et Mystica* (Rome, 1952), pp. 37–63; A. Benigar, *Theologia Spiritualis* (Rome, 1964), pp. 263–93.

20. Cf. L. Mendizábal, *Annotationes in Theologiam Spiritualem* (Rome, 1962), pp. 113–24.

21. The same process is related in other parts of the NT: Acts 15: 14; 18: 10; Rom. 1: 25; 2 Cor. 6: 16; Tit. 2: 14; 1 Pet. 2: 9–10; Rev. 21: 3.

22. Right at the outset of his activity, Jesus called his first followers, who immediately became a group. It was a relatively large group, not limited to the Twelve (cf. Mt. 8: 21; 27: 57; Mk. 4: 10; 10: 32). This group is clearly distinguished from people in general (Mt. 9: 10; 14: 22; Mk. 2: 15; 3: 9; 5: 31; 6: 45; 8: 34; 9: 14; 10: 46). Apart from purely occasional circumstances, Jesus did not speak to individuals. His preaching was always to the group or to the people. Jesus did not set up an office of spiritual direction for the sanctification of individual souls. Such a project would have been alien to his mission.

23. Ma. Angustias Moreno, *El Opus Dei, Anexo a una historia* (Barcelona, 1977), p. 61.

24. Ibid., pp. 61–62.

25. The theme of the 'leader' is constantly repeated in *The Way:* nos. 16, 19, 24, 32, 365, 411, 833, 931. The Spanish word *'caudillo'* is applied to the 'leader who directs and commands people, particularly in war' (M. Moliner, *Diccionario del uso del español,* Madrid, 1975, I, p. 559). Its usage in this book becomes even stranger and more un-evangelical when one recalls that it was written during the Spanish Civil War, in Burgos, the capital from which the *'caudillo'* Franco was directing his armies.

26. Cf. G. Therrien, op. cit., p. 1, quoting O. Cullmann, *Christ et le temps* (Neuchâtel-Paris, 1957), p. 164.

27. The central importance of this theme in spiritual tradition has been sufficiently elucidated by G. Bardy, F. Vandenbroucke and J. Pegon in their article, 'Discernment des esprits', in *Dict. de Spirit.* III, 1247–81.

28. St Ignatius of Loyola, the master of obedience, is a typical example. But his teaching was directed to those who had undergone the experience of the Spiritual Exercises, whose aim is precisely to teach discernment. The *Imitation* . . . also deals with obedience (I, 9. 1; I, 18. 4; I, 20. 2; I, 23. 4; III, 5. 7; III, 13. 1, 2; III, 49. 6), but always in the broader context of the spirit of discernment.

29. *The Way,* no. 53: 'What then—you ask, uneasy—of this critical spirit, which is as the substance of my character? Look—I will set your mind at rest— take a pen and a sheet of paper: write simply and trustingly—and, oh!, briefly—the reasons for your anxiety, give the paper to the superior, and think no more about it. He, who is your head—who has grace from his position—will file it . . . or throw it in the wastepaper-basket'. See also nn. 457, 798, 945.

30. Alienation appears precisely when a person uncritically identifies with an ideology imposed on him and not corresponding to either his personal experience or his real needs. As an introduction to the subject, v. E. Ritz, 'Entfremdung', in *Hist. Wört. der Philosophie,* II (Basle-Stuttgart, 1972), pp. 509–25.

31. *The Way* never betrays the slightest admission of the possibility that others might be as right as, let alone more right than, a confirmed member of the Opus. Its statements on the subjects of 'holy intransigence' are eloquent in this respect (nn. 393–99).

32. The poverty *The Way* recommends is a poverty 'of the spirit' (no. 631), perfectly compatible with possessions and even riches (no. 632). The means it suggests are, amongst others, spending what one has and what one does not have (no. 481), so that money ceases to be a preoccupation (no. 487), even using every available means (no. 488). That is to say, money should be used without this becoming a problem. Power and influence are measured by the same yardstick—cf. e.g., no. 63. Mgr Escrivá is deliberately not addressing himself to the common people, but to the intellectuals, those who direct and occupy positions of influence. He constantly emphasizes this.

33. Cf. J. I. González Faus, 'Las tentaciones de Jesus y la tentación cristiana', in *Estudios Eclesiásticos* 47 (1972), pp. 155–58.

PART III

Christian Life Today

Enrique Dussel

Discernment: A Question of Orthodoxy or Orthopraxis

DISCERNMENT is a constitutive and internal movement of praxis, not of an unconditional or absolute praxis, but of the real historical praxis, that is to say one conditioned and set in its situation. All praxis is the praxis of a social class in a process of social formation situated in space and time. Discernment as a practical moment cannot have its basic reference in a theory or theoretical expression, but in real human action within which it fulfils its own role, which it is our task to describe. We are not dealing with a 'hermeneutical circle' in which interpretation of discernment starts with a theory or verbal formulation; we are dealing with a 'practical circle' where the practical exercise of discernment is based on the very structure of action. Without room for doubt, discernment is an aspect of the structure of orthopraxis.[1] Let us now examine the question bit by bit.

SEMANTIC CLARIFICATIONS

The first task is to agree on certain questions of meaning if we are to be understood.

In Classical Thought

The question of 'discernment' was posed by Aristotle in his *Nichomachean Ethics*,[2] and by Thomas of Aquinas in the *Summa*.[3] Both saw discernment as a movement in prudent action concerned with judging not scientific, theoretical or speculative questions, but the particular acts to be carried out themselves. Discernment operates on the level of the probable practical, the occasional, the doubtful about which there can be no security, evidence or certainty. This makes it a moment of prudence and related to prophecy.[4] As a practical moment, discernment is not understanding of ends or principles, nor is it properly speaking deliberation to reach a decisive practical conclusion (*hypólepsis*),[5] but a judgment (*krísis*) requiring *separation* (or break) from immediacy (hence the Latin root *cerno* or the German *sondern*) distinguishing between courses to be carried out according to their *sense*.[6] Discernment (*diákrisis*) is therefore an act, a virtue and a charism but all linked to action, to praxis,[7] and praxis in the future sense. Discernment is defined by temporality and contingency.

The 'Diákrisis Pneumáton' in the New Testament

St Paul's list of charisms includes that of 'the gift of recognizing spirits' (1 Cor. 12:10), which is therefore a gift of grace from the Spirit enabling us to distinguish clearly in actions and in persons what is conducive to the building of the kingdom. In Hebrew this process of recognition was expressed by the word '*mishpat*' which indicated an act of judgment proper to God himself (1 Sam. 24:13). Essentially, discernment is the discovery in action of the presence of one of the two 'spirits': 'this is how we can tell the spirit of truth from the spirit of falsehood' (1 Jn. 4:6). 'It is not every spirit, my dear people, that you can trust; test them, to see if they come from God; there are many false prophets now in the world' (1 Jn. 4:1). The spirit of falsehood, the devil, is revealed by the false prophets. Discernment then is primarily occupied in distinguishing between true and false prophets (Mt. 7:15; 24:11; 24:24; Lk. 6:26; Acts 13:6; 2 Pet. 2:1; Rev. 16:13; 19:20; 20:10). The Holy Spirit helps to discover the same spirit through charism.

Discernment and Ideology

As discernment is a practical judgment, it operates precisely as a statement relating to praxis; hence it has an ideological status. Its ideological compass is not that of ideas in their theoretical function, but in their function of legitimization or critique of praxis.

Fetishized practical judgment. In the proposition 'I discern', the subject (I) is not an unconditional absolute as Fichte claimed at the beginning of his *Wissanschaftlehre* (1794), an ontological expression of the lack of consciousness of all the conditionings inevitably at work, *a priori,* in every human, finite, real 'I'. In reality before this 'I discern', this 'I' is *already* linked to some form of work (being a medieval knight is not the same as being a serf, a business executive is not the same as a worker), and a certain set of social relationships (it was not the same to be a Roman senator as to be an anonymous member of the *plebs*) which determines (though never absolutely) that the 'I' is part of a social class. This class has its own interests or objectives. Praxis, as is well known, is determined by its end; hence the class interest or end constitutes every moment of action. Discernment as a moment in the practical-prudent act (*recta ratio agibilium*) is determined by class interests, by its class *situation.* Without their noticing it, the dominant classes in a social structure will in practice operate their discernment along lines identified with the interests of their domination. In the history of the Church (as in the case of Latin, Byzantine, Muskovite or Latin-American colonial Christendoms), we can see that the ecclesial judiciary institution has sometimes been confused with the ideological apparatus of the State. So, in the Latin Middle Ages or in colonial Latin-American Christendom, the Holy Inquisition set itself up as a tribunal through which the dominant social order of the time could be reproduced and legitimized. In this case the judgments proceeding from discernment tend to become constituted as laws; the consciousness of their relationship with the dominant order is lost and they become fetishized, absolutized; it would seem that they are valid forever beyond history. In this process the interests of the dominant class are fetishized, not merely as their natural interests, but as divine interests.

Practical, historical judgment. On the other hand, when the 'I discern' is set in its true historical process, we understand that the conflict of discernments (of the 'two' Spirits) originates in sin, in domination, in the fetishistic claim to legalize an order of domination forever. Therefore, if this 'I' is linked with the popular classes, the dominated, the oppressed, the emerging, the 'poor', the class discernment is immediately unfetishized or made historical (whether this class discernment is that of pre-Christian religions, such as those of the Roman Empire, or Christian ones, such as those of feudal structures or contemporary capitalism). The conflict of class interests (domination-oppression) or national interests (centre-periphery) is the cause of conflict of discernments. In the early days of Christianity, as all believers were members of the classes oppressed by the Empire, intra-ecclesial discernment took the building of the kingdom as its criterion. The gnostics were therefore discerned as a practical deviation from the faith because they sought to disincarnate Christian requirements. Later on, however, the interests of the ruling classes came to be mixed in with, or rather to cover over, the interests of the kingdom of heaven, and—hard to discern—an ideological structure arose. The practical, historical judgment of the prophets was often interpreted by the Church-institution as belonging to false prophets.

A First Description

We could then conclude that discernments as a charism is a practical moment in liberating prudence [8] whose function is prophetic criticism of the fetishized judgment of rulers and discovery through its own considerations and judgments the practical steps necessary if the poor and the oppressed are to fulfil their historical interests and those of the kingdom. Recognizing 'spirits' is knowing how to distinguish between the spirit of liberation of the lowly and the spirit of oppression of the powerful.

OTHER NECESSARY DISTINCTIONS

This first description is not enough in itself, we need to widen our analytical framework if our later, particular analysis is to have an outcome even though it is only through examples.

Tactical, Strategic and Eschatological Discernment

Discernment as practical judgment refers to mediations; it is essentially situated on the tactical level, that of actions which have to do with parts of actions but not with the whole; it is concerned with means and not with ends. However, from the stand-point of Christian faith in the eschatological kingdom, the ends or strategic structures themselves become mediations (since the eschatological is the final end: the strategic goal of all strategy). This is why we have not only to discern the basic setting of tactics in strategy (since the criterion or principle—$\dot{\alpha}\rho\chi\bar{\eta}$—of action is the end and therefore the basis of the judgment made by discernment), but we must also consider if the strategic goal (for example the capitalist or Socialist system as a whole) is the one best suited to the aims of the eschatological kingdom in the *here and now* of Christian praxis. A false strategic choice can overlay the judgment of a tactical decision; believing that the kingdom is already manifest in the present system (legitimization of strategic domination) equally overlays and removes the possibility of strategic criticism of the system as a whole (the origin of the reforming approach).

True discernment therefore requires an adequate appreciation of the connections between the tactical, strategic and eschatological levels. Right judgment (*rectitudo* or ὀρθός) depends in the final analysis on the eschatological decision: 'Let the good news be brought to the poor!'; which on the strategic level requires historical systems in which the poor live in justice; which, in turn, requires this or that action on the tactical level.

The Double Meaning of Orthodoxy and Orthopraxis

The original meaning of the word 'orthodoxy' has undergone a certain shift of emphasis. Through modification of its original content (which related to practice and history), it has come to mean a body of doctrine ('*sana doctrina*' in Augustine, *De vera religione,* V), dogma, or a body of articles of faith that have to be believed (Vat. I, Sess. III Ch. 3) proposed by the Church to the faithful, and then even something explained by: 'revealed dogma proposes *objective* knowledge', and therefore the theologian should oppose all 'systems contrary to this *objective* value of dogma'.[9] Dogma or the theoretical-orthodox structure thereby possesses a 'substantial changelessness of meaning'.[10] These formulations allow the interpretation—which is not to say that they require it exclusively—that orthodoxy should be interpreted as a body of theoretical expressions which can be confused with the very structure of the dominant ideological formation. Orthodoxy would therefore be a theoretical and objective formation disconnected from the praxis that produced it in the first place.

Given this concept of orthodoxy, whatever is opposed to it is heterodox (the practical judgment of the poor as an emerging class will therefore be considered heterodox—as happened in the case of Jesus and Hidalgo, as we shall see), and orthopraxis will come to follow from and be based on orthodoxy, so orthopraxis becomes the praxis based on, and at the same time conforming to, an *a priori* fitting theoretical formulation. In the theoretical concept of orthodoxy, orthopraxis is *a posteriori*. Furthermore, if this is the case, discernment becomes a theoretical act of mere 'application' or deduction from theoretical principles to objective realities. We are in fact here faced with a fetishized manipulation of practical judgments raised to the level of doctrines pretending to universality. We are exactly on the level of the 'δόξα ἀνδρός.

If, on the other hand, orthodoxy is the true manifestation of the Glory of God: 'so that they may see the Glory (δόξαν) of mine which you have given me' (Jn. 17:24), the epiphany of the honour of Yahweh, then this orthodoxy can only be discovered in praxis itself. The Glory of God is expressed in his Son; and the Son is expressed in his 'flesh' and in his Spirit. The 'ortho-doxy' of the Father is expressed in history through his Son, whose practice brought him to death on the cross and is expressed in his Church and in his poor by his Spirit. Discernment of the true manifestation (orthodoxy) of the Spirit in praxis in service of the poor (ortho-praxis) is a consequence and not an antecedent. It is *a posteriori* and not *a priori* to the practical choice by the Spirit in his poor. It is not so much the *class situation* of him who discerns that matters; what matters is rather the *position* he takes up, whether from choice or birth, with regard to the oppressed classes. If one is through birth or choice prepared to see the interests of the poor as his own interests (the absolute criterion of orthopraxis: 'I was hungry and you gave me to eat'; that is the definitive principle of divine discernment in history, in 'he will separate [ἀφορίζει] some from others', Mt. 25, 32, 35), one's practical discernment originates on the eschatological horizon of faith and on the historical horizons of strategy and tactics—all moments of praxis itself—and not in theoretical, universal abstract propositions. On the basis of orthopraxis (or service to the poor), orthodoxy (or the manifestation of the Glory of God in the poor) discerns the praxis of domination of the ruling system as heteropraxis, and the orthodox doctrine for ideological formation of the ruling class still legitimized by religion as heterodox.

SOME CONCRETE ANALYSES

Let us take three examples from the history of the Church: the praxis on which our faith is based, that of Jesus Christ, a situation from the early nineteenth century that clearly illustrates our theme, and a practical choice facing many Christians in Latin America which demonstrates a reformist discernment based on conformism to strategic interests (which are neither eschatological nor tactical).

Christological Discernment

Here we should try to put ourselves not in the situation of the 'I' of Christ and the way in which he himself discerns (the criteria of *his* discernment, which is that of God, are set out in the texts already quoted in Part 1, section ii, amongst others), but in the 'I' of the disciples (an anticipation of the subject of the discernment of the Church and of our own discernment). When Jesus asked his disciples: 'who do men say that I am?' (Mk. 8:27), he poses the question at the root of all Christian discernment.[11] The disciples have to recognize the 'Spirit' of Christ. For discernment to take place, there has to be a break or separation from daily reality so that praxis can be clarified by praxis itself: 'they went out into the villages of Caesarea'. The practical judgment the Lord was asking them to make could be made on the basis of comparison with existing models of prophets or messiahs; the existing models were those orthodox in the Jewish tradition. This is why the disciples, without yet committing themselves, said: 'Some say John the Baptist and others Elias . . .', they trot out the various orthodox models in this way, but when the Lord has them with their backs to the wall and asks for their personal opinion, Peter exclaims: 'You are the Christ'. Jesus's reply is somewhat disconcerting: 'he forbade them to tell it to anyone'. Why did he require this silence?

Christ did not refuse the title that Peter gave him but he certainly refused the 'content' which the disciples would give to such a title. The *orthodox* and traditional messianic models of Israel were in open contradiction to the unique way in which Jesus wished to live his messianism. Jesus was to fight this orthodoxy and this is why he forbade them to speak of the matter, but he goes straight on to begin to pull down the old orthodoxy and replace it with a *new* orthodoxy: 'and he began to instruct them: this man will have to suffer much . . .' (Mk. 8:31). The *new* orthodoxy (absolutely heterodox for tradition, for the Pharisees, the priests and the disciples themselves—hence Peter's protest and Christ's rejection of the temptation of Satan in Mk. 8:32–33), is announced from the standpoint of a *new* praxis (heteropraxis for tradition and, of itself, the reason why Jesus was condemned: 'all without exception pronounced sentence of death' Mk. 14:65). That is, Jesus' new orthodox teaching was opposed to all the orthodox teachings traditional to Israel and still in force; this new orthodox teaching, this new concept of messianism, stems from a new structure of orthopraxis that was to lead him to his death and which the ruling religious groups discerned as heterodoxy. This is the crux of our theme. Jesus condemned the dominant orthodoxy from the standpoint of the new orthodoxy based on the poor. Jesus's praxis was condemned as heteropraxis because it opposed the dominant structures and thereby brought in a new practical structure, the orthopraxis of the kingdom which will judge all human praxis till the end of time.

However, the disciples did not learn the new orthodox model theoretically, nor were all Jesus' words and preachings enough. It was only the praxis of his life, death and resurrection that gave them discernment: 'how foolish you are and how slow to believe what the prophets foretold!' (Lk. 24:25). Discernment comes later than praxis and springs from it! The orthodox teaching of the early Church, heterodox for the Jewish people which did not accept the new messianism of Jesus, was produced from the orthopraxis of the Son who gave up his life to bring the good news to the poor.

From the moment when Christ identified himself with the oppressed ('taking on the condition of a slave', Phil. 2:7) which meant taking up a very clear *class stand* in a peripheral province of the empire, he demonstrated the point of origin, source or fount of orthodoxy (the manifestation of the Glory of God); orthopraxis as service to the poor, radically opposed to the dominant orthopraxis of the system. Imitating the orthopraxis of Christ—the heteropraxis of the system—means taking on the interests of the poor and making them our own. This praxis of service is the practical principle of discernment: 'I was hungry and you gave me to eat'. But giving the hungry, the poor, the oppressed classes, the exploited countries food to eat is heteropraxis, change, revolution. If you serve the oppressed, you cannot serve the system. The praxis of liberation of the exploited, the orthopraxis of the kingdom of Heaven, is subversive praxis for the Prince of this world. But Jesus' teacher, his mother, had already shown the orthopraxis of the kingdom as heteropraxis of the world: 'he has put down the mighty from their throne and exalted the humble. The poor he has filled with good things and the rich he has sent away empty' (Lk. 1:52–53).

The Heterodoxy and Heteropraxis of Miguel Hidalgo y Costilla

Let us now look at the example of the political liberator hero of Mexico, who with San Martín and Bolívar, freed Latin America from the colonial rule of Spain. Miguel Hidalgo (1753–1811), who had based his studies on the inspiration of the Enlightenment and the Catholic tradition that was responsible for the emancipation of the Hispano-American creoles, took up arms on 15 September 1810 against the Spaniards. On that day Miguel Hidalgo, acting as parish priest of his community in Dolores, rang the bells which used to call the faithful to the liturgy, to launch the cry of rebellion against the oppressors. He had been director of the theological seminary in what is now Morelia and his views on independence had led to punishment by his bishop (orthodoxy judging praxis), and being confined to his small distant parish of Dolores. When Hidalgo, some little time later, had become General-in-Chief of all the freedom fighters; when thousands of popular soldiers, many of them Indians, were going from victory to victory and it was feared that the capital itself would fall, the Mexican bishops pronounced a formal sentence of excommunication (his heteropraxis was declared and he was cut off from the ecclesial community), and the faculty of theology declared in a public statement that Hidalgo had fallen into heresy (heterodoxy). Can one ask for a clearer case? The liberating hero is declared heterodox and heteropractical! What was the response of this Catholic priest and political hero? It was this:

I swear to you then, beloved fellow citizens of mine, that I have never strayed one iota from the belief of the Holy Catholic Church . . . Be sure, beloved fellow citizens of mine that if I had not undertaken to free our kingdom from the great evils that oppressed it [liberating orthopraxis considered as heteropraxis] and from the many far greater ones that threatened us, I would never have been accused of being a heretic [liberating heteropraxis producers, in the eyes of those who condemn him, doctrinal heterodoxy] . . . Open your American eyes, do not allow yourselves to be seduced by our enemies: they are only Catholics through politics; *their God is money,* and the only object of their combined forces is oppression. Do you perhaps believe that he who is not subject to the Spanish despot cannot be a true Catholic? From where does this *dogma,* this *new article of faith* come? [12]

Hidalgo, now acclaimed as a hero by all, including the Church, was a clear living example of recognition of 'spirits': he was able to withstand being declared heterodox and excommunicated by the ruling classes—and by the whole institutional Church. In 1811, his head hung from the battlements of the fortress of Guanajuato. Liberating orthopraxis (subversion or heteropraxis for the ruling system), had been judged once more as heterodox, and yet Hidalgo is the founder of the new strategic-historical order we call Mexico, and those who condemned him have been erased from the memory of the people. Hidalgo's discernment, integrated into a praxis that sprang from love of the oppressed, was based on better criteria than those of the bishops of his period, and those of the theologians of the biggest theological faculty in the whole of America. The prophet is praxis, his discernment has become the measure by which all the rest are judged, but through the 'logic' proper to the kingdom, the orthopraxis of the Gospel will always be subversive heteropraxis for the ruling, dominating, present system.

The Roman Pontiff himself has been known to connect his discernment with the ruling praxis of European monarchies and thereby commit a double error of discernment. In the encyclical *Etsi Longissimo* of 30 January 1816, he condemned the emancipatory revolution in Latin America. He regarded the revolutionary praxis, which 'has been so bitter to our heart', as heteropraxis; he advised the bishops to demonstrate 'with all zeal the terrible and most serious prejudices brought about by the rebellion'. And still on 24 September 1824, when Mexico itself had been freed from Spanish colonial domination, the encyclical *Etsi iam diu* condemned liberating praxis once again: 'we have received the dreadful news of the deplorable situation to which both the State and the Church have been reduced by the scourge of rebellion in these regions'. No one in the Church is exempt from committing the error of false practical discernment (which should be distinguished from infallible definition, but this is another question). Europe is a long way from Latin America and with events like the Third General Conference of Latin American Bishops in Puebla (October 1978) in their minds, Christians committed to the poor and the oppressed do not have any great confidence in the practical judgment of those who spend their day among books, diplomats and the great ones of the world, far from the oppressed classes of the peripheral nations . . .

'Third World' Discernment in the Context of the Ideology of the 'Trilateral Commission'

Discernment is always occasional, tactical or strategic. It is always limited by its contemporary historical context. When the Latin American, European or North American Church adopts a particular stance, it 'discerns' the 'signs of the times' in one way or another. Its interpretation of the signs is necessarily linked to its practical choices, its class options, in accord with the system as a whole (strategically capitalist or socialist, for example). There are not really three positions. Many, however, insist on adopting a 'third position'. This third position in the context of capitalist expansion, following the crisis of 1973 and based on the directives of the 'Trilateral Commission' [13]—which in many respects has taken over from the aims of the 'Club of Rome' embodied in European capitalism—takes shape as a reformist and, at best, developmentist 'discernment' of the capitalist ethos (which is not strategically questioned but merely improved in detail—at least in intention). A European theologian tells us that: 'the activism of the revolutionary years is no longer in fashion, but it will not be possible to stop introducing energetic *reforms* within the established order'.[14] If this reformism is still understandable at the 'centre', it is totally inexplicable on the 'periphery', where huge masses of unemployed and under-employed cannot be integrated into a system of systematic exploitation. A social scientist has described the Latin American situation in these terms: 'either there is a decisive revolutionary advance towards Socialism and a way of development and progress for the great masses of our peoples is opened up, or there will be recourse to the barbarity of fascism, the only means by which capital can safeguard its political survival'.[15]

When a way is claimed—as is done by social democracy or Christian democracy—to be neither capitalist nor Socialist, in fact since the claim is made from within the capitalist world, it is the opposite (Socialism) that is denied and a reformist developmentism adopted, an 'ashamed' capitalism.

Nothing suits North American foreign policy better than this stance if it is to overcome the recession produced by the military dictatorships in Latin America in alliance with the multinationals, so as to be able to impose '*restricted* democracies' according to the ideology of the Trilateral Commission. Christianity thereby plays imperialism's game.

The Church, as an institution, has adopted a 'political tactic': faced with the militarist States of Latin America, it seeks to reserve a 'relative autonomy', to avoid being merely an 'ideological apparatus of the State', and to remain within 'civil society'. Therefore it denies State Capitalism and through its criticism of the doctrine of 'national security' (as in the case of Brazil), it keeps its distance, its prophetic capacity and its relative autonomy. The real question arises when this '*political tactic*' (neither capitalism nor socialism) is raised to the level of *strategic* theory (orthodoxy), thereby closing the door to strategic criticism of the oppressing system. When this happens, the 'political tactic' of survival falls into reformism and plays the system's game: it condemns revolutionary heteropraxis as heterodoxy. Jesus never condemned the Zealots (although in fact they were merely reformist guerrillas) because by doing so he would have legitimized the Roman Empire and its oppression!

The question deserves to be examined at greater length but I merely introduce it here because, in my view, it is one of the central questions in the application of discernment to Latin America today.

THE ORGANIC LINK BETWEEN DISCERNMENT AND PRAXIS

Discernment is not theory, but like theory it must link itself 'organically' (that is adequately and through institutions) to orthopraxis if it is to be a true discovery of orthodoxy as the revelation of the Glory of God in the poor.

Linking discernment to the praxis of the liberation of the poor and the oppressed *organically* (orthopraxis properly so called), requires that the act of interpretation or clarification be carried out from a class position truly rooted in history and reality. Only the Christian who is *in some way* in a correct class *position* (not necessarily making a romantic sacrifice but definitely making a real choice in favour of the interests of the oppressed classes with all the risks this implies) can discern the actions practiced by the system 'from below'. He can thereby distinguish the praxis of domination from that of liberation.

Discernment is not a private or individual act; it is an act of the Church, of the community; it is a co-responsible act. Therefore, reference to historical, popular, political praxis of the oppressed classes (first level), and of the Christian community committed to this (second level), opens the way to orthodox discernment (third level). In practice, the *locus* of discernment would not seem to be private 'confession', nor even the 'Chapter' of the religious orders or 'spiritual direction', since all these *loci* can be organically disconnected from the praxis of the poor in their process of liberation. The *locus* of discernment today would seem to be the 'revision of life' as practiced in the Base Communities.[16]

In the base community, the real presence of Christians belonging to the oppressed classes permits discernment of reality *from* the standpoint of the poor, the hungry and the exploited. Furthermore, the community as a group commits itself to the struggle of the people. This *class position* adopted by all the members of the community, even if they are middle class or belonging to some other class, allows them to place their own 'I' organically or truly in the 'We' of the people, of the poor. Discernment therefore has a correct origin. Orthodoxy is discovered in interpretation based on the orthopraxis of the poor. If the act of discernment is disconnected from its organic link with the political praxis of the oppressed classes and the peripheral nations (the poor of all nations and the poor of the world), this discernment will lack real models or criteria, concrete historical ones on which to base its estimative interpretation. Its view will be clouded over, blinded, led astray and erroneous.

CONCLUSION

The process of reviewing daily life (revision of life), the praxis of the Gospel in the light of faith, with the community of believers collaborating in testing this praxis to discover whether or not it is orthopraxis, organically linked to the struggle of the oppressed classes for their liberation, would seem to be today the place in which the charism of 'recognition of spirits' is to be found. Discernment takes its valorative criteria and the possibility of judging the orthodoxy of life from praxis, with its goals and interests.

Those who claim to recognize spirits with the help of their individual conscience alone, on its own, will in the end find only the interests of the ruling class, the criteria of an orthodoxy that justifies its own orthopraxis—unfortunately merely the ideological formation of the ruling system and its oppressive praxis. The only guarantee that discernment can be truly and historically orthodox—therefore heterodox for the rulers—is for it to be linked to the praxis of the liberation of the poor—orthopraxis which is heteropraxis for the oppressive system—in which practical judgment has its beginning and its end.

Translated by Paul Burns

Notes

1. On discernment as a charism, see my article, 'Differentiation of Charisms', in *Concilium* 109 (1977), pp. 38–55. On the general theme, see H. Assmann, 'A Praxeology of liberating faith in the world', in *A Practical Theology of Liberation'* (London & New York, 1977). On more specialized aspects of the question, there are articles to be consulted, such as: Kittel, 'διάκρισις, δόξα, πράξις,' etc. in *ThWNT;* 'Discernment', in *DTC* IV, 1375–415, by Chollet; Martin-Pegon, in *DS* III, 1285ff; 'Unterscheidung der Geister', in *LTK* X (1965), p. 330; Dublanchy, 'Dogme', in *DTC* XI (1911), 1574–650; 'Orthodoxy', in *The Cath, Ency.,* XI, p. 330; etc. On exegesis, see *The Bible and Liberation: Political and Social Hermeneutic* (Berkeley, 1976). On Christology, F. Belo, *Lecture matérialiste de l'évangile de Marc* (Paris, 1974). In general, O. Semmelroth, 'Orthodoxie und Orthopraxie', in *Geist und Leban* 42 (1969), pp. 369–73.

2. 'Discernment . . . is not to be confused with knowledge nor with opinion . . . Discernment is not concerned with the eternal and immutable, but with what is becoming. It is centred on questions where there is doubt and deliberation. It is concerned with the same questions as prudence . . . Discernment only has a critical character . . . Discernment can judge the matters prudence deals with' (*Et. Nic.,* 1142 b 34–1143 a 15). See my 'Para una destrucción de la historia de la ética' in *Ser y tiempo* (Mendoza, 1973), pp. 39ff; also, *Filosofía ética latino-americana,* sec. 31, 'El *ethos* de la liberación' (Mexico, 1977), on the whole question of prudence in liberation.

3. For discernment, 'importat iudicium rectum non quidem speculabilia, sed circa particularia operabilia, circa quae etiam est prudentia' (II-II, 51, 3 resp.). Cf. *In Et. Nic. com.,* L. IV, lec. IX, n. 1235ff.

4. Cf. II-II, 171ff.

5. *Et. Nic.,* 1140 b 11–20.

6. In fact, discernment is not so much σύνησις as γνώμη. But the former clarifies the latter. On γνώμη, see *Et. Nic.,* 1143 a 19ff and II-II, 51. 4: on the charism, I-II, 111, 4 resp.: 'Et haec sunt contingentia futura, et quantum ad hoc ponitur prophetia; et etiam occulta cordium, et quantum ad hoc ponitur *discretio spirituum'*.

7. 'All that is to be found in the realm of action . . . [πάντα τά, πράκτα]' *Et. Nic.* 1143 a 33.

8. See *Filosofía ética latino-americana,* ch. V.

9. Dublanchy, 'Dogme', 1579–81.

10. Ibid., 1602.

11. See the excellent article by A. Castillo, 'Confesar Cristo el Señor: Ortodoxía y Ortopraxis', in *Christus* 481 (Mexico, 1975), pp. 19–31.

12. See my *Religión* (Mexico, 1977), pp. 199–203.

13. Cf. the series on *Carter and the Logic of Imperialism,* ed. H. Assmann, Vols I and II, with contributions by C. Furtado, N. Chomsky, F. Hinkelammert, M. Bonino, J. L. Segundo and others (San José, Costa Rica, 1978). The 'Trilateral Commission' is a group of 'wise men' from N. America, Germany and Japan, that has been meeting since 1975. Its work has been accepted by President Carter, who was a member of the commission before running for

President. Its ideology is aggressive and expansionist, seeking to put 'a more optimistic face' on imperialism. Faced with the collapse of the 'Alliance for Progress' of the 1960s and the impoverishment of the peoples of Latin America by the military dictatorships (backed by Kissinger), it proposes the creation of internal markets and distribution channels, the struggle for 'human rights' and the installation of 'social democracies' or 'strong, restricted democracies' (i.e., ones that can be manipulated).

14. H. Küng, *Christ Sein,* I, 3, c (Munich, 1974).

15. Th. dos Santos, *Imperialismo y dependencia* (Mexico, 1978), p. 471.

16. See my articles 'The Base Community in the theology of liberation', in *Concilium* 104 (1975), and 'Differentiation of Charisms', att. cit. The limitation of a work such as J. Habermas, *Theorie und Praxis* (Frankfurt, 1971), is that although it deals with the function of organization (in e.g., 'Historisches zur Organizationsfrage', pp. 37ff), it does not explain how this ties in with the *most real* form of praxis: that of the oppressed classes.

Not long ago, I was speaking to Bishop Vieria Pintos of Nampula in Mozambique, who explained to me that, in that Socialist country, his diocese was wholly organized into base communities. It now has more than 7,000 adult catechumens. The base community decides which of its members shall join the Communist party of Mozambique to carry out its patriotic function. Once a member of the party, the person chosen gives an account of his actions to the community in the 'Life Review'. Here the three levels are perfectly linked: *First,* political praxis with the revolutionary people; *Second,* Christian praxis in the base community; *Third* (that is, in third place, after the other two, *a posteriori*), Christian discernment of orthodoxy in orthopraxis.

Enrique M. Ureña

Christian Discernment, Psychoanalysis and Marxist Analysis

'FIDELITY to the past consists not in mere repetition but in its ever-new proclamation of word and deed. If it is to go on meaning the same, what we receive from the past has continually to take on forms of expression suitable to the age at once accommodating and contradictory. To be faithful, fidelity must take account of the ceaseless transformation of the world'.[1] I would like to apply this incisive observation of Horkheimer to the theme of Christian discernment. Our faithfulness to this classic practice of Christian spirituality can only be maintained through ever-new considerations of it. Only through these can Christian discernment continue to mean the same thing.

All the articles that make up this *Concilium* are really contributions to this necessary revitalization and reinterpretation of Christian discernment. My own contribution will concentrate on something that at first sight may appear a mere play on words: we must seriously *discern* if specifically *Christian* discernment still has a separate meaning today. The need to pose this question today has an indisputable rationale: basic and pre-eminently influential currents of modern philosophy claim to have demonstrated the meaninglessness of any religious statement or its reductibility to purely mundane meanings.[2] If these views are accurate, it is clear that any Christian discernment would in fact be reduced to pure discernment *on its own* and this would mean the internal collapse of any attempt at bringing a specifically *Christian* discernment 'up-to-date': fidelity to such discernment would then consist in the expression of its self-dissolution.

The historical materialism of Marx and the psychoanalysis of Freud are without doubt at the head of two of the foremost currents of contemporary thought. I therefore propose to make primary reference to them in this 'discernment' of Christian discernment. This article will have two well-differentiated parts. In the first, I propose to examine the critiques of religion made by Marx and Freud in the context of their respective interpretations of the historical development of human society and with the critical aim of examining their inner coherence.[3] In the second part, having critically asserted the right for a religious consciousness to survive even in our days, I will go on to some considerations of the form in which, after Marx and Freud, we can today embark on a process of Christian discernment. The arguments in this second part will be illustrated by reference to a specific and very relevant case: the Christian discernment of whether it is possible to choose a Marxist-Socialist society.

CRITIQUES OF RELIGION

Freud and historical maturity

Freud's critique of religion forms an essential part of his own application of his psychoanalytical theory to an interpretation of the historical development of human culture. Towards the end of his life, in January 1936, Freud wrote to Romain Rolland describing how he had tried to apply psychoanalysis first to himself, 'then to others and finally, in a daring leap (in Kühnem Übergriff), also to the whole human race'.[4] In a few lines I can obviously not enter into a full discussion of the springboard for this 'daring leap', this jump from theoretical elaboration of clinical experiences with neurotic patients to an interpretation of the history of humanity. The springboard is many-sided and complex.[5] I must limit myself to a summary presentation of what a systematic internal examination leads me to believe constitutes the basic link between psychoanalytical theory in its strict clinical sense and Freud's interpretation of the historical development of human society.

Freud decided relatively early on that the Oedipus complex formed the inner core of neurosis.[6] However, his clinical practice often showed him that the reactions of the neurotic patient to his parents in the Oedipus complex and the castration complex seemed to lack sufficient justification in the patient's individual history and therefore could only have a philogenetic explanation. On the basis, then, of ample clinical material, of his study of dreams and of the legends and mythologies of primitive peoples, Freud came to the conviction that 'the archaic inheritance of man not only includes dispositions but also contains mnemonic traces (*Erinnerungsspuren*) of the life experience of earlier generations'.[7] This picture was completed by the investigations of Darwin, Atkinson and Robertson-Smith into the historical origin of the human species, which provided him with the basic 'archaic life experience', transmitted from generation to generation through the supposed 'mnemonic traces': the sons of the primitive tribe and desired women whom the father-chief had reserved exclusively for himself. The father of the tribe had then been tyrannical and brutal with his sons, and finally, the sons had discharged their aggressivity by assassinating the father.

In the Oedipus complex the child, according to Freud, would be merely repeating the original philogenetic event on an individual basis: individual infancy repeats the infancy of humanity thanks to the mnemonic traces handed on from generation to generation. This discovery, which Freud regards as enormously important, would then provide the decisive systematic link which makes possible the daring leap from the interpretation of individual neurosis to an interpretation of the whole human race—the belief that Freud spoke of in his letter to Romain Rolland. Freud himself tells us that this leap is something *inevitable* [8] since it means that individual neurosis is now explained in its turn by reference to this historico-universal hypothesis.

This philogenetic re-reading of the Oedipus complex should be complemented by the parallel re-reading of another concept closely linked to it and also basic to psychoanalysis: the concept of the superego.[9]

Freud constantly defines the superego as 'the heir to the Oedipus complex': [10] the heir because it arises out of the disappearance of this complex. The superego internalizes the relationship with the father in the son: you must be like your father but you cannot do what your father forbids you. In reality what the father forbids him is nothing other than what the father's own superego forbids him, and the paternal superego thereby becomes the agent passing on all the prohibitions accumulated from generation to generation since the institutionalization of the first moral norms. This institutionalization arose for the first time in history, according to Freud, after the assassination of the father of the primitive tribe by his sons. This assassination gave rise to remorse and the impulse to identify with the murdered father. The brotherly clan then internalized the prohibiting function of the father through totemism: exogamy was introduced and it was forbidden to kill the totemic animal which represented the father. Freud claims that religious, ethical and political institutions were born in this way as a reaction against the historico-universal Oedipus complex and a help in overcoming it; they are therefore its 'heirs'. These institutions grew from generation to generation, with new moral norms (to the extent that society developed and became more complex), to become the 'superego of humanity' and it is they that have the final say in forming the individual superego. There is therefore a socio-historical explanation for this as well as for the Oedipus complex.

The historico-universal re-reading of the Oedipus complex and the superego allowed Freud to see cultural development as a process of growth in humanity marked by neurosis. Before we can put this concept of Freud's into a clear form, we need to look briefly at his concept of neurotic repression.

According to psychoanalytical theory, neurotic symptoms can only be interpreted by placing them in relationship with a similar event which occurred during the development of the libidinous function of the individual in early infancy.[11] At this stage of life, when the ego is still very little developed, libidinous impulses can act with such force in quest of their immediate satisfaction as to overcome all possible resistance by the still weak ego. If the ego is incapable of *rational* control of the impulse in question, it has no other recourse than that of *repression* (the desymbolization and burial of the impulse in the unconscious). The impulse repressed in this way still carries its affective and blind charge and appears in its true colours in the neurotic symptom tyrannically ruling the patient and forcing him into pathological behaviour. The patient can only free himself from this tyranny if he succeeds through psychoanalysis in drawing the previously repressed problem up into consciousness and thereby seeing that what formerly appeared an insoluble problem is now, for the strengthened mature ego, mere 'child's play'.[12] We can now sum up how Freud saw the development of human society as a process of growth for humanity, marked by neurosis, needing psychoanalytical therapy in its adult stage.

According to his schematic framework, in the infancy of humanity, man found himself faced with a problem he was not then capable of resolving *rationally:* that of dominating his aggressive and sexual instincts on the altars of cultural development. In the face of his impotence, he had no other recourse than to resolve the problem *pathologically.* Moral and social rules, which arose with religion in totemic society, made living in community possible, thereby preventing the repetition of the brutal murder that marked the dawn of humanity, but these rules, as this summary shows, were not originally based on reason. In the first place, they were consecrated with a mystical and mysterious halo, a blind affective charge, as something that had to be accepted blindly with no possibility of rational examination: morality

owes this tyrannical characteristic, according to Freud, to its 'dependence on religion, its proceeding from the will of the Father'.[13] Religious morality is therefore a neurotic morality: it obtains its irresistible
and oppressive force from the enormous affective and historical charge
it possesses; it is the symptom of a past and 'repressed' event in the
history of humanity.

But, according to Freud, humanity has now entered on the era of its
maturity. The problem posed by culture (the domination of aggressive
and sexual instincts) is now capable of being resolved rationally
through a sort of 'psychoanalytical reflection' on a universal scale.
Religion, in the guise of universal neurosis, was necessary during the
infantile period of humanity, but in its adult phase, the conflict between
culture and human instincts has to be resolved rationally. To para-
phrase Freud's famous formulation for the individual ('the ego must be
formed from the id'), we cay: 'rational morality must be formed from
religious morality'. This would be Freud's recipe. This would constitute the 'psychoanalytical cure on a universal scale'. Man must reject
as irrational and oppressive a whole series of moral norms which derive
their strength only from 'religious-neurotic' morality, and must formulate other moral norms based rationally on social need and not on
divine command.

The Freudian critique of religion is therefore part of his evolutive
interpretation of human society, part of his theory of culture. His
atheism could therefore be summed up like this: the rational maturity
of the human being coincides with the disappearance of religion. Before going on to Marx, I would like to quote a passage from *The Future
of an Illusion* which in the context of the foregoing considerations acts
as a summary of the meaning of Freud's critique of religion and of the
form in which Freud sought a scientific basis for it. He writes: 'we
know that the individual is incapable of achieving the step to culture
without passing through a more or less clear phase of neurosis. This is
due to the fact that the child cannot repress many of the instinctual
requirements which will later be of no use to him through rational
reflection and therefore has to neutralize them through acts of repression . . . in the same way, we must accept the idea that the totality of
humanity in its secular development falls into situations analogous to
neurosis; and for the same reasons: because in the times of its ignorance and intellectual weakness, it could only achieve the instinctive
rejections necessary for human beings to live together through sheer
affective forces . . . religion is the universal human neurosis and, like
that of the child, derives from the Oedipus complex from the relationship with the father. This framework indicates that the abandonment of
religion must take place with the fatal inevitability of a process of

growth and that we find ourselves now just in the middle of this phase of development'.[14]

Marx and Political Economy

The critique of religion made by Marx is found mainly in his early writings. This is understandable if one bears in mind that between 1837 and 1844, Marx took an active part in the polemics surrounding the philosophy of Hegel. In view of the essentially religious undercurrents in Hegelian thought,[15] this debate necessarily had a strongly religious tone. In his later writings there are very few substantial references to religion and these are lost in the vast sea of tens of volumes. So Marx's critique of religion is not integrated in his concept of the historical development of human society in such a direct way as is the case with Freud,[16] even though on its deepest level it is also inseparable from this concept, as we shall go on to see.

Historical materialism is the great theoretical framework within which Marx sought the dynamic laws governing the development of human society. His critique of political economy [17] forms the basic and decisive part of his theory of historical materialism. This is why it occupies a primary place in the overall context of his writings: from 1844 onwards, Marx devoted his studies almost exclusively to economics and related problems.[18] The reason for this concentration on political economics is well known. From Hegel, Marx learned that man's historical achievement is a product of his own labour [19] and that the logic of the various ways in which human society is organized must be sought in the logic of the development of the means of production in relation to different forms of property.[20] So Marx tried to build a theoretical model of the development of human society based on a theoretical model of the development of the *economic* structures of this society. In order to do so, he had to change from being a philosopher to being an economist.

The interpretations of the historical development of human society in Marx and Freud are therefore differentiated by being closely linked to two different positive sciences, economics and psychology respectively, despite the many common characteristics thay share as a result of a common philosophical inheritance. The basic difference is that Marx saw the dynamic of the development of society as lying primarily in the dimension of the relationship between man and external nature (the dimension of the means of production), while Freud laid most stress on the dimension of the moral rules governing social relationships between men. Returning to the theme of their critique of religion, it is clear that this had to play a lesser part in Marxist thought since his study was basically concerned with the economic functioning of Capitalist society.

If this is the case, how then can one speak of Marxist critique of religion as inseparable from his interpretation of the historical development of human society? In my view the following text gives a deep summary of his critique of religion and answers the question: 'The suppression of religion as the illusory happiness of the people is the requirement for their true happiness. The need to put an end to illusions concerning their own situation is the need to put an end to a situation that requires illusions . . . Criticism of heaven thereby becomes criticism of the earth. Criticism of religion becomes criticism of law and criticism of theology becomes criticism of politics'.[21]

Together with a strictly historical critique of religion, that is one referring to particular forms taken by religion and to its ideological use as an oppressive force used by the ruling classes to the detriment of the oppressed classes, Marx also criticizes religion on a deeper and more strictly philosophico-historical level: he sees religion as a plant that can only grow in the rotten ground of a society disfigured by the exploitation of man by man, a plant that will simply cease to germinate when the underlying situation of the society has been changed, when oppressing and oppressed social classes have disappeared and human beings are then able to realize themselves in the fulness of their social being. Since Marx saw the key to this transformation of a class society, of this 'situation that needs illusions', as lying in the economic undercurrents, from 1844 onwards he devoted all his strength to a theoretical study of the capitalist economy with the practical intent of encouraging and providing a scientific basis for the revolution that was to lead to Communist society. Marx did not return to a long consideration of the plant but only of the rotten ground in which he saw it growing.

Marx's *atheism,* implicit in this deeper level of his critique of religion, can then be seen to resemble that of Freud: the full humanization of man coincides with the disappearance of religion—or, to use terminology more like that of Marx himself: religion belongs exclusively to the prehistory of man.[22] In this sense, Marx's critique of religion is inseparable from his historical materialism as an interpretation of the development of human society. It is inseparable, not so much because it is systematically interwoven into this interpretation, as is the case with Freud, but because it is one of its basic starting-points.

These two interpretations of the historical development of the human race, though tied to different analytical techniques and different empirical sciences, coincide in being atheistic interpretations of man in a very particular sense: they reconstruct his history following a logic and a dynamic of development pointing toward a fulness of man, characterized amongst other things by the total disappearance of all idea of religion; religion appears to be justified only as something necessary to the human species during the 'neurotic' or 'prehistoric' stage of his growth process. By reducing the meaning of the religious phenomenon to purely sociological and anthropological levels in this way, the very possibility of a specifically Christian discernment disappears of its own accord: man, once entered on the stage of his historical maturity, cannot use any other form of judgment in order to make decisions concerning the practical direction of his individual and socio-political life than one consisting of purely rational discourse without any reference to contents that transcend his earthly history.[23] We must now go on to ask how far these two critiques of religion are internally coherent.

Both Marx and Freud in fact limit themselves, by a process of reduction, to considering the moral and political applications of religion.[24] Their critical condemnation of the ideological and oppressive characteristics that have accompanied and still accompany moral concepts based on religious traditions, and of the religious or quasi-religious justification of particular political and economic structures, is one of the great achievements of the critiques of both Marx and Freud, but religion also has another purpose (which can be analyzed by philosophy and sociology), consisting in responding to the basic and permanent contingencies of individual existence: sickness, death, loneliness and guilt.[25] The internal and radical incoherence of both critiques of religion has to be seen, in my view, in that they both move illogically from their critical unmasking of the ideological character of religion in its moral and political purposes to its purpose of responding to the basic, permanent contingencies of human life. But it is precisely this historical development of human reason that, having reached the stage of maturity or adulthood, has produced a critical philosophy rightly seen by both Marx and Freud as irreconcilable with all ideology and all universal neurosis, that has enabled us to see clearly that these basic contingencies of human life, unlike moral rules and the rules governing socio-political organizations, do not respond to and cannot be resolved by this same maturity of critical thought.[26] This is where religious consciousness finds its purest nucleus and its perennial right to existence: a right that has to be respected by critical philosophy, since this very philosophy pruned the leafy tree of religion till, with all superfluous branches cut away, the original trunk stood revealed. The stage at which man reaches his rational maturity does not coincide with his *atheization* but with the *maximum purification* of his religious consciousness. This purified religious consciousness will prevent man from idolizing his own beliefs and hopes, will prevent him from using them in the service of ideology and oppression and will open up to him the *possibility* of accepting the message of a man who claims to be God, who announces salvation and fulness despite the imperfectibility and irrationality of this earthly history, who announces a resurrection beyond death. Taking some fine words from Adorno's *Negative Dialectic*, one might say that this purified religious consciousness is what has to keep alive: 'the experience that thought which does not behead itself opens out to transcendence till it reaches the idea of a world constituted so that not only will it have put an end to all sorrow, but in it the irremediably past will be remedied'.[27]

A SPECIFICALLY CHRISTIAN DISCERNMENT

We can now move on to the second part and ask how, after Marx and Freud, it is possible to conceive of a specifically Christian process of discernment. As I said at the beginning of this article, I propose to base my considerations on a particular example: the Christian discernment of whether it is possible to choose a Marxist-Socialist society as an alternative to a Capitalist society. The choice of this example starts from the supposition that Christian discernment today should be extended to the public and communal life of believers, to their political decisions, and not be restricted to the dimension of the so called 'spiritual life' or 'inner life' of pious souls.

Now that Marx and Freud have formulated their critiques of ideologies [28] and particularly after the 'pruning' process of their critiques of religion, the Christian has to realize that, in the first place, he cannot discern directly from 'theological criteria' or from 'criteria of faith' which of the two choices before him corresponds to the 'will of God', which choice proceeds from the 'good spirit' and which from the 'evil spirit'. In its first stages, the true Christian process of discernment cannot be distinguished in any way from the true discernment of any other non-believer: these first stages have to consist of a philosophical and sociological, political and economical analysis of the two alternative forms of organizing our industrialized society (or, where applicable, an underdeveloped society), which will provide a certain degree of evidence as to which of the two forms of organization promises to be more human, freer and more just. This type of analysis clearly has to take into account not only the pure ideals of Capitalism or Marxist Socialism, but also the particular historical situations of societies in which these pure ideals will be put into practice: is it an industrialized or an underdeveloped society, is it already a Marxist-socialist society or a Capitalist one, what is its socio-cultural basis and what moral and valorative systems apply to the majority of people in this society and so on? If *this analysis* leads to the conclusion that in a particular historical situation, the introduction of Marxist Socialism would produce a more human, free and just society, a more rational society economically and a more democratic one politically than any, Capitalist alternative, then the Christian, just like the non-Christian, would have to opt for *this* Marxist-Socialist society. The same is of course true if the opposite conclusion is reached. Up to this point there is nothing specifically Christian in the process of discernment. These considerations, however, do not exhaust the question of discernment since it is clear that no sociological, political and economic analysis can eliminate possible discrepancies with regard to the judgment one makes of what is 'more human, free and just'. So, for example, after serious political and economic analysis (which is unfortunately absent from most discussions on the subject), some will judge that the repression and irrationality incorporated in the political and economic structures of great Capitalist countries are more inhuman and more unjust than those built in to the structures of the countries of eastern Europe, while others will come to the opposite conclusion.

So what criteria can be applied to a final judgment on what constitutes greater liberty and greater justice? In my view the psychoanalysis of Freud and the critique of ideologies of Marx make it no longer possible to absolutize particular structures as objectively incorporating inalienable values of freedom and justice (for example, the sacred and inviolable right to private property). Since Marx, any moral and political system hides the suspicion of an oppressive ideologization. Furthermore, since Freud, any consensus on a particular moral or political system hides the suspicion of a *false* consensus, a neurotic or systematically mutilated communication. Since both Marx and Freud, therefore, the Christian who believes he has reached the point of choosing Marxist Socialism by virtue of the requirements of liberty and justice imposed *by his faith,* by virtue of the *evangelical* call to the liberation of the poor and the oppressed, must seriously suspect the possibility of the fruits of his choice being ruined by the maggots of a change from one oppressive and despotic ideology to another (the change from an ideologically bourgeois Christianity to an ideologically Marxist Christianity). Equally, the Christian who believes that Marxist Socialism must be definitely rejected by *virtue of his faith* and of the respect for freedom and justice demanded by it, must seriously suspect if the fruits of his choice will not be eaten by the maggots of unspoken materialistic interests—the fear of losing privileged economic, social and political positions and a secret respect for money rather than the human dignity of his fellow men. If this is the case, what then are the specific criteria for a *healthy Christian* discernment in the example under consideration? [29]

These criteria can only refer to the formal conditions of the very process of Christian discernment. The particular choices arising from this process cannot, as we have just shown, be justified by criteria of their 'suitability' to particular 'objective' Christian moral values, but in the final analysis can only be considered valid in a Christian sense by reference to the formal approach the Christian makes to the process of discernment of which they are the fruit. What then is the specifically Christian formal approach that will guarantee a healthy process of discernment, one guided by the 'good spirit'? In the classical terminology of St Ignatius, this attitude is one of *indifference:* not wanting riches above poverty, longer life rather than a shorter one, health rather than sickness, etc.; that is, it is the attitude of one who only really hopes for salvation and fullness beyond death and who is therefore *free* to seek *justice* above all ideology and all particular interests. His approach will therefore be anchored in that 'purified religious consciousness' that is the fruit of a critical re-reading of the critiques of religion made by Marx and Freud.

This concept of a Christian process of discernment as something consisting not in removing subjective obstacles in order to achieve knowledge of 'an objective truth' (a 'will of God') already made outside ourselves, but as a process in which this truth and will of God becomes known in the course of their coming about, supposes a critically overt admission that we possess no *external* criterion guaranteeing our faithfulness to God. It supposes explicit and conscious acceptance of the *theoretical obscurity* of our faith and the *practical opacity* of our sinful life.

Psychoanalysis and Marxist analysis can make our faith hesitate, but they can also help us to understand the whole of our Christian life more clearly as a long journey through an endless process of discernment, through a discernment in which the 'good spirit' is what continually prevents us from falling into the greatest temptation posed by the 'evil spirit': the temptation of seeking a pre-emptive possession of the 'good spirit' and therefore believing ourselves free at every moment from the influence of the 'evil spirit'. Psychoanalysis and Marxist analysis can help us to see that *Christian hope* is the opposite extreme of the sin of trying to *idolize* God in order to manipulate him at our will and thereby feel *secure*. Psychoanalysis and Marxist analysis can, in a word, help us to understand that the discernment of truth is, for the Christian, nothing other than the *truth of his discernment* in the same way that the meeting 'with God in this life is nothing other than our tireless search for him'.

Our attempt to redefine Christian discernment by confronting it with psychoanalysis and Marxist analysis has brought us at the end of the road to results quite in keeping with the most solid Christian spiritual tradition. Fidelity to the past has thus been kept in an open and critically receptive dialogue with two of the currents of thought which,

explicitly or implicitly, have made the greatest contribution in our time
to the ceaseless process of transforming the world.

Translated by Paul Burns

Notes

1. M. Horkheimer, *Zur Kritik der Instrumentellen Vernunft* (Frankfurt,
1967), pp. 350ff.

2. By 'religious', I mean here, non-problematically, everything that implies a
reference to something transcending this earthly history (God, the other life
. . .).

3. I obviously cannot produce all the evidence for my arguments in the space
of this article. These are supported by other studies of mine: *Karl Marx,
Economista* (Madrid, 1977); *La Teoría de la Sociedad de Freud* (Madrid, 1977);
La Teoría Crítica de la Sociedad de Habermas (Madrid, 1978); *Le Crítica
Kantiana de la Sociedad y de la Religión* (at press); *Kritischer Theorie und
Christlicher Glaube: Eine Auseinandersetzung mit J. Habermas* (Frankfurt,
1975); 'Marx and Darwin', in *Hist. of Pol. Economy* 9, No. 4 (Winter, 1977);
'Ideología religiosa e ideología política' in *Sal Terrae* 66 (1978), pp. 263–71.

4. S. Freud, *GW* XVI, p. 250.

5. See my study on Freud, op. cit.

6. See Freud, *GW* V, pp. 127ff; VII, p. 428; VIII, p. 50; IX, pp. 42, 188ff; XI,
p. 349; XII, pp. 213, 226, 237ff; XIII, p. 413; XIV, pp. 82ff.

7. Freud, 'Moses and Monotheism', in *GW* XVI, p. 206.

8. Ibid., p. 207.

9. This would have to be complemented by a re-reading of the feeling of guilt.
But we can do without that at this point.

10. Freud, *GW* XIII, pp. 264, 277ff, 380, 399; XIV, pp. 85, 254, 304; XV, p.
70; XVII, p. 137.

11. We have already seen how the Oedipus complex underlay neurosis.

12. Freud, 'The Question of Lay Analysis', in *GW* XIV, p. 233.

13. Idem, 'Moses . . .' in *GW,* XVI, p. 230.

14. Idem, 'The Future of an Illusion', in *GW,* XIV, pp. 366ff. See also *GW*
XIV, pp. 362 and 432; XV, p. 181.

15. See, e.g., the magnificent study by M. Theunissen, *Hegels Lehre vom
absoluten Geist als theologisch-politischer Traktat* (Berlin, 1970).

16. Neither Marx, nor for that matter Freud, devoted any treatise specifically
to religion.

17. By 'Critique of Political Economy' I mean here the whole vast corpus of
Marx's economic works, not just the one that bears that title.

18. This is what makes Marx a milestone in the history of economic thought.
See my study on Marx cited in n. 3.

19. K. Marx, *Ökonomisch-Philosophische Manuskripte* (1844), in *MEW* 13, pp. 8ff.

20. Marx, *Zur Kritik der Politischen Ökonomie, MEW* 13, pp. 8ff.

21. Idem, *Zur Kritik der Hegelschen Rechtsphilosophie. Einleitung,* in *MEW* 1, p. 379. There is a similar page in *Zur Judenfrage, MEW* 1, p. 352.

22. Lenin was to make a note fully in accord with this view: 'Religija = rebjatschesctvo, dersctvo tschelovetschestvo' (Religion = infancy, the childhood of humanity), in *K. Marks, F. Engels, V.I. Lenin o religii* (Moscow, 1975), p. 269.

23. See E. Ureña, *La Teoría Crítica de la Sociedad de Habermas,* op. cit.

24. This characteristic is clearly anticipated in Kant. See my study on Kant cited in n. 3.

25. J. Habermas, *Legitimationsprobleme im Spätkapitalismus* (Frankfurt, 1973), pp. 162–65.

26. Idem, *Philosophisch-Politische Profile* (Frankfurt, 1971), p. 197.

27. T. Adorno, *Negative Dialektik* (Frankfurt, 1966), p. 393.

28. Comparison between Psychoanalysis and Marx's critique of ideologies has been made in many forms. See Ch. 3 of my study on Freud, in n. 3.

29. The philosophical background to what follows, which really requires a careful development beyond the scope of this article, is inspired by Habermas.

René Simon

The Moral Law and Discernment

WE must not underestimate the importance of discernment in the field of morality. Though the term is not very often met with, and in theology is ascribed largely to 'spiritual' discourse by virtue of a kind of division of labour which would allow moral theology the discussion of precepts and 'spirituality' and the investigation of the paths of perfection, the reality that it reflects is to be found in the notions of 'the heart', moral consciousness, prudence and the theory of moral illumination in Augustine, and nowadays in the determinative question of moral criteria, and so on. Discernment is an essential and complex aspect of ethical concerns. Its complexity results from the associated necessity of rational analysis and motivational evaluations, consideration of the emotional affectivity of the individual, the effects of his life-history, his environmental and class affiliations, and his philosophic and religious allegiances. In this regard, discernment is always committed and draws its strength not only—and not even mainly—from the cold precision of scientific reason, whatever its magnitude, but from the human and spiritual quality of the individual in question.

Hence any complete examination of the concept should include all the aspects mentioned hitherto. The title of the present article, however, restricts my endeavour to a study of the connections between the moral law and discernment. I shall remain within these bounds, and divide my thoughts into three sections: an historical account of the Thomist theory of prudence, or of what might be called prudential discernment (this theory is striking for its richness and extreme boldness); the externality of the moral law, its universality, and its relation

74

to authority, power and institution; and the theological aspects of the problem. My reflections are conceived on a formal level, and are more often concerned with the Law in its formal nature as Law—its legality in fact. Whenever laws (in the plural) are in question, I shall use instead the term 'norms'. [1]

PRUDENTIAL DISCERNMENT IN THOMIST THEORY

In Thomist teaching, prudential discernment can refer to the judgment of the duly informed conscience in so far as it is affected by the virtue of prudence. The dual qualification of prudence as an intellectual virtue and a moral virtue, on the one hand, and the recourse of Aquinas to the Stoic theory of the association of the virtues, on the other hand, give prudential discernment its characteristic complexity and universality. *Recta ratio agibilium,* or prudence, is, in fact, in the realm of action what 'mode' or 'art' is in the realm of making: that is, the rightness of practical reason, with however the difference that it requires not only the *bonum opris* but the *bonum operantis.* This directly implies in the moral agent the rightness of 'appetite'. In the Thomist view, the rôle of prudence is to know in order to direct and order (*imperare*); it can only do so in conformity with preordained ends. These ends are those of human life: that is, they derive from fundamental values on the basis of which are organized temperance, fortitude and justice, which together with prudence comprise the four cardinal virtues. Prudence cannot decide the means of attaining to these ends unless their usual 'intention' is ensured by the moral virtues. In this perspective, it seems the virtue proper to initiative and daring. Discernment cannot rest content with a foundation consisting of the legal and juridical virtues, institutional worth and power, and the purely factual regulations of any particular society. Prudential discernment is critical both in an anthropological and in an axiological sense.

The theory of the association of the virtues tends in the same direction. It reveals the fact that discernment brings into play the entire complex of virtues. The notion may be outlined thus: 1. there can be no prudence without the moral virtues; 2. there can be no moral virtues without prudence; 3. the possession of any one virtue implies the possession of all the others, and all of them are wanting if any one of them is wanting.[2] This thesis indicates clearly that prudential discernment is much more than the work of speculative reason. It is inscribed in the depths of being and brings into play those basic options which supply man with the ultimate motivation for his actions. Here we are faced with the question of the dialectical relation between theory and practice (*praxis*), unless we deprive the two concepts of their too one-sidedly Marxist derivation and allow the first the meaning of rigorous reflection on practice which integrates at one and the same time the scientific analysis of those factors conditioning action, its anthropological interpretation and its ethical evaluation; and if we understand the second, practice, not primarily as production and making, but as acting, not *facere* but *agere*, not *poïen* but *prattein*. In this view prudential discernment is located at the interface of the two terms, theory and practice.

The moral quality ensured by discernment in the practice of decision and action is not without a certain motivational daring, nor without the risk of possible error. Though human ends are relatively determined, the variety of means for their realization is a function of the all but infinite complexity of actual situations and unusual circumstances, of individual and collective history, and of the psychological make-up of each individual human being.

Furthermore, discernment is closely and necessarily connected with the moral law, before all else, because in the primary principles of the natural law it affords the structural basis of the very possibility and operation of that law. We know that in Thomist theory the absolutely primary principle is represented as a kind of *a priori* ethic: *bonum est faciendum, malum vitandum.*

Moreover, it is significant that the elucidation of the prime precepts of natural law leads St Thomas, once he has formulated the fundamental principle I have just mentioned, to distinguish 1. a law of conservation, corresponding to the tendency of all being to preservation within its own existence, 2. a law of fertility, corresponding to the tendency of the living being to multiply the species, a law of the person, corresponding to the tendency of the rational being to live as a reasonable being: that is, to acknowledge its radical dependence on God and to live in society. What is remarkable is that in those categories that have tended to obsolescence, St Thomas formulates in the first two precepts something analogous to the two taboos of murder and incest which modern anthropology and psychoanalysis locate at the very basis of society, culture, and morals as the conditions for their very possibility, and as the foundational structures of the humanity of mankind. This is all the more surprising since the order of the Thomist argument puts the precept of sociability in third place, as if to stress that it owes its existence to the other two. We may deduce that the ordered unity of these elementary precepts arises from formal frameworks or dynamic schemata (Maritain), and extends into the network of norms and rules of ethical life, the content of which may vary with time and place. The foundation of discernment in the Law is therefore an essential component of the Thomist viewpoint. This analysis might be extended with a reflection on the externality of the Law, which is not lacking in the thought of Aquinas. But there is no room for it here, and instead I shall examine it in the context of contemporary thought.

MORAL LAW AND DISCERNMENT

Externality of the Law and Discernment

It may seem paradoxical to introduce the concept of externality in order to discuss the connections of the Law with discernment, inasmuch as it is precisely the externality of laws that would seem to offer ground for criticism. However, the matter demands closer analysis.

It would be easy in fact to show, in an historical study of ethical or political theories, how permanent this problem is. That is not necessary here, however. I shall remain content with a brief account of the problem from three angles: from the politological viewpoint, from the psychoanalytical and ethnological viewpoint, and from the philosophical viewpoint.

In an article on totalitarian experience and political thought,[3] M. Gauchet, supporting the thesis that social division 'is neither derivable nor reducible', but 'aboriginal', devotes a short passage to the Law. He asserts that it amounts to a constitutive externality, to a location which is precisely the place of law, from which point the social whole derives significance and shape as a whole. That would be possible only if men forbid themselves or are forbidden to occupy that place and to lay hands on it. Hence the Law is no one's property: 'It is because the Law is beyond everyone that it is valid for everyone'. Understood at this level, the Law (which is not to be identified with laws) may be defined as 'the empty form of what is the same for all'. And the specific law (the norm) obtains its legality only from its capacity of ensuring in the actuality of relations, behaviours and forms of practice, that existence which is both common (the same) and differentiated (all) on the basis of an aboriginal division. The individuals in a certain group and the group itself exist only by virtue of the necessity of their subjection to the Law, or by the impossibility of their not being so. Externality may be grasped only in terms of a certain transcendence which religions have always associated with the Deity.

To put this in other words, we may say that the Law depends on the two taboos of incest and murder. These allow the construction of a differentiated universe of individuals. The interdiction has in fact a dual rôle: that of forbidding, of closing the way to the desire in you to kill; and that of self-identification with the immediacy of impulse, abolishing the distance between you and it, between you and the Other. To give in to that desire would amount to allowing room for the undifferentiated chaos of generalized violence which would mean the death of individuals and unregulated sex. The function of the interdiction is primarily to delimit, to differentiate, and to locate individuals and objects and thus to overcome a generalized confusion that would imply the death of individuals. The interdiction which in its aspect of interdiction is the aspect which renders impossible the coincidence of self and self, and the self-reflective reduction of the Other to the Same, opens the door, in its positive dimension, to undefined possibilities of discourse between partners in the same human venture and in common action. In this context the Law is never anything other than the controlled assignment of our differences or, which comes to the same thing, the controlled encounter and recognition of our desires and freedoms.

Lévinas' original idea is to see in the relation of Otherness the constitutive relation of the human individual. The fundamental experience is the experience of the Other who allows himself to be recognized as the being who is inalienable, irreducible to the laws of the Same, noncodifiable in juridical, economic, political categories, and unassimilable to the objectivity of scientific knowledge. The entry of the Other into the universe of myself cracks the identity of the self and puts in question its happy spontaneity. The countenance of the Other, a countenance which speaks and which expresses itself, denies all possession and all power: 'The expression which this countenance introduces into the world does not defy the weakness of my powers, but my power of power'.[4] The moral Law is nothing other than the address of the epiphany of countenance to me, both on the basis of its poverty and on the basis of its transcendence or its majesty (as Lévinas puts it).

Here we have three different conceptions. They have in common their revelation of the externality of the Law as one of its fundamental traits. It is at this level that we should first locate any reflection on the association of the Law and discernment.

1. First, discernment (far from being set against the Law) is, when understood thus, on the contrary at the frontier of decision and action, and the outcome of the Law. It relies for its prime truth on continuance in the direct line of foundational externality, of constitutive Otherness, and of its capacity to retain that openness to the Other, which is always initial and never terminal. That makes it capable (and this is the other aspect of discernment) of denouncing, criticizing and rejecting what in practice would be rendered impure by customs and institutions—the irreducible difference of the Other.

2. In these conditions, discernment does not (as far as its very roots are concerned) arise from a knowledge of the objective and scientific

kind. Undoubtedly, both scientific and technical results and methods comprise a necessary aspect of discernment, because they are an indispensable part of a rigorous and effective approach to situations and action. Scientific and technical reason enters more than ever today into the determination of possibilities, but it renounces any ultimate judgment on the desirable and preferable. Discernment is primarily a matter of an ability to assume the 'incomprehensible limitation imposed on the desire of another who has been accorded the same degree of existence as oneself (and) the irrationality of love to which in the end any reason trying to account for the irrational difference of beings must have recourse'.[5]

3. This relation to Otherness, or this externality of the Law, means that discernment must be ready to go beyond the fine arrangements of ethical codifications and their coherence, in order to accept the possibility of ambiguous choices and the possibility of unjustifiable options in accordance with the closed system of our values and our ideas. 'The irrational act by which one says No', says Jankélévitch, 'resembles a hatchet blow. This action is a passionate thing, a violence which is not always harmoniously integrated with our past and our social context'.[6]

We have to maintain both the sharpness of the decision which cannot attain to the slowness of deliberation, and the necessary verification which reintroduces a non-definitive coherence into the manipulation of our values. Hence the normative formulations of our behaviour-patterns are always subject to the non-objectifiable nature of Otherness, and to the unutterable externality of the Law. Nothing can dispense the individual from assuming his responsibilities, from taking risks, and from risking himself. The risk of discernment is in fact a double one. There is first the risk of discernment itself, which is never absolutely self-assured, thanks to the disproportion between the infinity or the elevation of the Other and me. The truth of the choice to be taken, of the just action which is to be undertaken, is always affected by this inevitable inadequacy. Then there is the risk of the individual: I risk *myself* in the action of discernment, because neither the best norms nor the most critical commitments, nor the richest communal roots, can dispense me from undertaking on my own account analysis, evaluation and decision—the means to action. Discernment is always a venture. Moreover, the individual takes yet another risk: He exposes himself, as it were: he makes himself vulnerable to critical opposition, to criticism, to attack. The supreme risk of death is, from this viewpoint, inherent in discernment, as is supremely apparent in the figure of the Suffering Servant.

Universality of the Law and Discernment

I have already mentioned the universality of the Law. I now come to the idea in its own right, because of its importance and because of its relation to the question of discernment. What arises here is the relation between the particularity of the subject (individual or group), and the law and the universal outlook of the Law. It shows that in its constitutive formality the law passes beyond the limits which it acquires from normative formulations and from its process of acculturation. Here we have another version of the original social division, of the subjective gulf, of the disproportion which is inherent in the relation of Otherness discussed in the foregoing.

This tension in the Law clearly has to do with discernment. I shall try to formulate this implication in the course of the following observations. The first effect of the Law would be to raise quite justly the particularity of discernment to a universal level, while leading the subject, in each of his manifestations, choices, and actions, to open himself to the countenance of the Other whose presence, as Lévinas says, is 'displacement, presence of a third (that is, of mankind as a whole looking at us), and the commandment which demands that we should take control'. Hence particularity and universality are closely linked, as may be seen from the Ten Commandments: they are proposed to all peoples in the ethical and religious particularity of Israel. This makes for tension, for the first recalls the necessity of actual roots or foundations, and the second runs the risk of sectarian restriction.

2. In regard to the first observation, we may say that discernment arises from the universalist dimension of the Law, which means that it can never rest content with purely deductive operation, as it has to derive evaluation, decision, action, *more geometrico,* from the style of an abstract rule which is never any more than approximate and inadequate to the transcendence of the Law. The universal does not exist; it has to be constructed on the basis of historically and culturally various individuals. On this level, the universal is to be deduced less from the normative content of the rule than from its formal ability to ensure the reception of differences and to favour the interaction of their qualities. Hence the aboriginal interdiction of killing, a supreme universal taboo, does not detract from the question of the means by which it is carried out. It is through the existence of these means, negatively set out in the commandment not to kill, that we eventually understand what killing means. Here discernment comes close both to the formality of the Law and to the concrete nature of action.

AUTHORITY, POWER, INSTITUTION AND DISCERNMENT

Law has to do with authority, power and institution. It is at the basis of the social order and of the due and peaceful co-existence of members of society. Hence it appeals to the mediation of the three above-mentioned instances. Power is on the side of the Law; it speaks in the name of the Law and from this point of view it is distinct from the rest of society. But that is not so much because it is possession of the law: 'It is on the side of the Law without being the Law'.[7] It is a perversion of the nature of power to identify oneself with it. As Gauchet maintains, power indicates an absence, an external location, the location of the Law, from which the location of the human community may be deduced. On this level we may say that the Law is not promulgated but promulgatory, not founded but foundational.

We may now see in what sense discernment is able to intervene. It is primarily associated with authority, power and institution, if we may say that these three instances indicate realities which are indispensable for the necessary social division and all that is characteristic of subjectivity as such. In this regard, discernment by its nature, the legitimacy of right, and also of fact, is characterized by authority, power and institution, whose function is not to impose ethical codes but to help the existence of a social location indispensable for the communal control of moral responsibility.

In this perspective, discernment can refute and deny any usurpation by authority and power of the Law for their own ends, or for any illegitimate identification with the Law. The instances of criminal submission to power which make this critical distance so very effective are still very close to us in time.

THEOLOGICAL DIMENSIONS OF THE PROBLEM

With the entry of Jesus Christ into human history, the Law was abolished neither in its original formulation not even necessarily in the normative formulations which had inhered in it. What if it were an integral part of creation? It would then be re-centred with unequalled power in the dual commandment to love God and one's neighbour. It would then win all its clarity from the naked dignity of the countenance of God revealed in the countenance of Jesus Christ, of that Otherness of whom Jesus is the sign and whose difference he incarnates and manifests in his distance from the practices of his time. He was the suffering and glorified Servant; he died because of his loyalty to the Father and his creative solidarity with mankind; and for that reason too he rose again to give himself in the Spirit a body which is the Church, whose mission would be to reveal the unassailable countenance of the God of the covenant. In this perspective, the Law, which is the Law of the covenant, has as its function its manifestation in the poverty of the one who has nothing with which to clothe himself, in the hunger of the one who has no bread, the thirst of the one who has no water, and the chains of the one who is deprived of freedom: the countenance of the Other, the cypher of the presence of Christ and his everlasting challenge to our responsibility.

In this context discernment is necessarily Christological. Jesus Christ, who united Grace, Law and Promise, remains for the believer the ultimate reference-point of his evaluation, decision and action.

In his earthy life and in his resurrection Jesus Christ showed the divine and human dimension of Otherness and in the Spirit endowed the impotence of the Law with the light and power of his Grace and Promise. The Matthean antitheses here reveal the thrust of faithful discernment; for they make manifest, in the transition from servile observance to responsible obedience, the presence of the countenance of the Other, to whom we must know ho to listen in his infinite summons to us—a summons which is threatened by murderous anger, sexual lust, discrimination against women, lying words and the precise 'adjustments' of the law of retaliation. The countenance of the Other is obscured in these actions. In these antitheses Jesus sends us back to the primary truth of the Law, which is the law of creation, itself comprised in the terms of the covenant. As for the resurrection, it is at least one of its possible meanings, and sends us back to the unassailable countenance of the Resurrected, who is irreducible to our reductive forms of logic. It returns us to the countenance and to the name of our neighbour whose otherness was already firmly pronounced in Genesis in the notion of the image, the image of a God who allows himself to be referred to by the name without a name of Yahweh.

Under these conditions, it is clear that Christian discernment must remain creatively open, beyond the normative forms of stability necessary to the physical existence of men in society; open, then, to the uncodifiable nature of what we may call the Law of the neighbour, the Law before all laws, of which Jesus in his life and death was an exemplary figure. This discernment should tend less to mere repetition and imitation than act as a stimulus to inventive responsibility.

One of the consequences of this Christian condition of discernment is that it can never accept uniformity, which would cancel differences. Openness to pluralism is congenial to discernment. Though the pluralism of the Christian churches is a sign of the historical inability to control differences in a Christian way, it is also a challenge—in the shape of current ecumenical endeavours—not to tone them down but to share their riches. Christian discernment should adopt these riches. We also have to extend this openness beyond the Christian sphere to the 'Jews' and 'pagans'. But how are we to experience in a Christian way the 'pagan difference' of human origins and the 'Jewish difference' of Scriptures common to us right up to the break introduced by the death and resurrection of Jesus? These 'differences' cannot be treated in terms of superiority. Election is a spiritual matter and reminds us here of our ethical responsibility before the manifest countenance of the Other and its mysterious symmetry with the countenance of Jesus Christ.

Loyalty to one's own tradition implies that discernment takes into account the necessity of an ecclesial verification of choices and actions, which would maintain the tension between Grace and the Law, charism and institution, and authorized laws and unforeseen innovations. This tension makes impossible authoritarian superiority and destructive anarchy, as well as appropriation by religious power of ethical regulations *and* the dilution of the ministry of unity entrusted to it. The control of practice has to be shared: the ethical responsibility of the believer is not solely a matter of the discernment of behaviour in regard to the peremptory prescription of authority. Discernment also has to do with responsibility at the level of prescriptions; this very responsibility is prescribed in the essence of the Law. Authority would lose its own authority if it did not acknowledge that.

Translated by John Griffiths

Notes

1. The typographical device of upper and lower case letters will ensure that the distinction is retained. In the passages on Aquinas I always refer to 'law'.

2. This is perhaps a way of saying that virtue and the virtuous man *hardly* exist.

3. M. Gauchet, 'L'Experience totalitaire et la pensée de la politique', in *Esprit*, 7-8 (June–August 1976), pp. 3ff.

4. E. Lévinas, *Totalité et l'Infini. Essai dur l'Exteriorité* (the Hague, 1961), p. 172.

5. D. Vasse, *Le Temps du Désir* (Paris, 1969), p. 136.

6. V. Jankélévitch & B. Berlowitz, *Quelque part dans l'inachevé* (Paris, 1978), p. 117.

7. Ibid., p. 188.

Josep M. Rovira Belloso

Who is Capable of Discerning?

INTRODUCTION

THE question may seem to present a simple moral issue but the variety of possible replies clearly implies many and deep differences concerning the spirituality and character of the Church, depending on the reply given.

It may be useful by way of introduction to summarize the possible replies without claiming to give an exhaustive classification. Some of these replies are of particular relevance today and some have been particularly relevant at one period or another in the history of spirituality:

(a) *He who is placed closest to the problems that require elucidation should discern.* This reply can be supported by one of the pontifical documents most closely concerned with expressing the responsibility of all the members of the Church: this is *Pacem in Terris,* and the following text, which may be literally somewhat obscure but is nevertheless important, is the relevant one: 'on the part of Catholics the duty of discernment rests in the first place on those who live and act responsibly in the community and in the particular sector in which such problems arise'.[1]

(b) *He who is closest to God can discern: the saint, the prophet, the person advanced in the spiritual life.* This is what we would call 'the response or illuminative way' and it undeniably has a long tradition. Only those experienced in the Spirit and its ways can discern, since 'the ways of God are not our ways' (Cf. Is. 55:8). This reply leads on to the second question of who is the saint, the prophet, the person well versed in the things of the Spirit.

(c) *The superior discerns*—since discernment must be practiced with practical guarantees of certainty and security and this practical security is achieved through obedience, which 'is never mistaken' as has so often been repeated in the religious life.

But it must be pointed out that discernment, which exists on the level of 'seeing' or of 'knowing', is one thing and obedience, which exists on the level of surrender of the will, is another.

(d) *The community discerns*—since it is the embodiment of the *'ecclesia ante et retro oculata';* it is the primary subject of the presence and impulse of this Spirit: 'if anyone has ears to hear, let him listen to what the Spirit is saying to the Churches'.[2]

This reply also brings new questions in its train: what do we understand by community? The local community, the local Church, the universal Church? And what specific rôle does the community play in discernment?

(e) It is important not to omit the reply which would point to experts on particular subjects as those who can and should discern. A good example would be a team formed around a catechist, a theologian, a psychologist, etc., acting as experts and therefore properly claiming a qualified degree of discernment.

The mere fact of enumerating some possible replies to the question indicates at least a part of the theological and spiritual substance implied by the question. Some of these replies already suppose a particular ecclesiological stance: in a verticalist ecclesiology those in authority discern; in a more horizontal ecclesiology—one that would set the People of God in pride of place—those who are closest to the reality or imbued with the charism of the Spirit proper to the situation, will discern.

After these preliminary sketches I need to tackle a necessary minimum of clarifications and distinctions to bring us closer to the centre of the question.

THE SUBJECT OF PRUDENTIAL DISCERNMENT

The word 'discern' suggests by its very etymology the action of choosing between two (or more) possibilities: seeing what is the true teaching, what is the right choice. This means that everyone is in a position where he has to discern; that is, to discover in a free and conscious form the motives for making a good choice. In order to choose well, it suffices for he who discerns to be prudent since—as Thomas Aquinas said—'counsel (or discernment preceding choice) belongs to prudence'.[3] Each and every man has to be prudent because all are called to choose and in order to do so, need to know how to discern.

Prudential discernment would seem to be an inalienable activity of free and conscious man, man capable of lucid confrontation with all the factors at play in a particular real situation.

Faced with reality, man works out his prudent and responsible decision: capable of 'responding' through a positive contribution to the world in which he moves as subject. Discerning in order to choose correctly is then a universally human function: proper to every responsible man who has moved beyond the stage of pure instinct such as nostalgia or ambition which produce an ideologized view of reality, or the stage of pure primary impulses. Discernment is a reflective activity proper to the spirit of man.

It is in this sense that I would subscribe to the first reply given in the Introduction, with this precision of meaning: every man is called to be responsible in the face of the problems affecting him and his world. In the light of this responsibility, man has to discern the most appropriate response—in the line of truth, justice and love—to the problems affecting his own being and his surroundings in such a way that through making these decisions, he comes to know himself: open to a relationship with others and placed in a particular set of circumstances. In this way the 'I', relationships and conditionings, become known in the act of discerning and transformed by the effects of the decision made. So man knows himself and so 'ex-ists'.

In this activity of knowing and deciding the Christian will generally not be acting alone. The local community and practices such as the 'life review' can be an excellent aid for this progressive growth in personalization and responsibility.[4]

This brief analysis of prudential discernment should be borne in mind as we go on to consider who should discern 'according to the Spirit'.

DISCERNMENT IN THE LIGHT OF THE SPIRIT

The next task is to find a deeper meaning of the word 'discern' and correspondingly a more specific reply to the question: 'who can discern?'

This would seem to open the door to 'illuminative response': those whom God illuminates are capable of discerning since they alone can with certainty interpret what is proper to God. The long road traced by this reply certainly has New Testament echoes: the Spirit of God, who illuminates man, is he who knows the plan of God, as is said in 1 Corinthians 2:10–11. But it was not till the time of Thomas Aquinas that the 'illuminative way' was described with the master's customary precision.

Who then is capable of rightly discerning the teaching or choice most in accordance with God's plan and action? The reply given by Thomas Aquinas in *Contra Gentiles* is: 'he whom God has illuminated with a certain inner and intelligible light which elevates the mind so that it can perceive things that understanding cannot perceive through its natural light'.[5] The logic of this reply, which St Thomas goes on to develop, is as follows: there is in spiritual discernment an element which is not only unknown, but which cannot come under the observation of the senses; it belongs to faith, which deals with what we cannot see. This unknown element, which cannot of itself be observed by the senses or grasped by the intelligence, is God loving and acting in our life: the presence of the Word and the direction of the Spirit.

If we are to discern or 'see' this element, we therefore require illumination from God himself: gratuitous and 'revealed' illumination as with Peter, who was able to discern that Jesus was the Christ because the Father and not flesh and blood had revealed it to him.[6]

However, if we are not to take this doctrine of illumination too mechanistically—as though it were a mere 'infusion' of light without reference to any observation of the visible signs present in reality—we should remember the essence of the understanding of faith as expressed by St John: the signs give witness; the light we receive in our innermost being attracts.

THE RELATIONSHIP BETWEEN 'PRUDENT' AND 'SPIRITUAL' DISCERNMENT

Is this clear distinction between prudential or 'natural' discernment and supernatural discernment, between the natural light of understanding and the inner light revealed by God, too far-reaching? The distinction is made in all Scholastic theology and there is no point in hiding this fact since it still has a useful purpose today: establishing the basis for natural discernment ('*gratia non tollit naturam*') can serve to put Christians on their guard in the face of doubtful spiritualizations and open their eyes and intelligence to the reality surrounding them. On the other hand, there may be better grounds for suspecting the distinction: the Thomist emphasis on the inner revealed light can seem alien to the problem of the connection existing between the signs—including 'the signs of the times'—and the inner light. In everyday life 'natural' elements such as health, aptitudes, human relations, possible harm to third parties, can all be interpreted as more or less specific signs of the will or call of God. These are signs that both hide and manifest the will of the Lord: perhaps his presence or his action.

It would then seem that the pure 'illuminative life' tends to place evangelical discernment above the prosaic common matters of every-day life; even above the dramatic field of decision-making in which the Christian, torn by inner struggles, is called to make decisions at the crucial moments of his life according to the Gospel. The 'illuminative life' must be seen in relation to prudent and realistic judgment. If not, there is no way of telling if this prudent judgment should precede, coincide with or serve to verify the inner light.

This is why we need to examine a new problem: what relationship exists between prudence, which opens one's eyes to all the factors involved in a particular situation, and the discernment of spirits, placed on the level of grace and the light given by God to man.

Here too, history can help us to find an intelligent balanced and Christian reply. The early Fathers introduced the concept of prudence as the base, regulator and limit of discernment. This is where discernment came to be called 'discretion': that is, good judgment and moderation in the things of the Spirit. So, when Cassian established 'moderation' as the regulating guide of spiritual demands; [7] when the Desert Fathers appealed to moderation (*sophrosine*) to psychological observation and practical wisdom as reference points in spiritual progress; [8] when the *Apophthegms* tell us that lack of measure (*metron*) is the cause of spiritual disaster; [9] when Basil says repeatedly that 'moderation is best in all things'; [10] when these Fathers, who in their own lives were hardly ignorant of the moment of pure abandonment to the Spirit, emphatically recall the role of '*metron*' or measure, this means that they are seeking to establish a dialectical connection between this moment of surrender to the Spirit and the moderation that comes from wisdom and practical experience. Ignatius of Loyola also expresses the relationship between illumination of the Spirit (such as he experienced in the episode by the river Cardoner near Manresa) and different states of mind, particularly consolations and desolations, which here play the part of 'moderation', capable of evaluating the impulse that seizes a man when he is moved by the Spirit.

APPRENTICESHIP IN THE SPIRIT AND APPRECIATION OF REALITY

We can now form the following conclusions:

1. The Christian is called to follow an apprenticeship which will show him the ways of the Spirit.

The only way out of the sort of tautology implied by the *a priori* assertion that 'those whom God illuminates are capable of discernment' (i.e., the saint, the prophet, etc.) is through an indication of the real and practical ways by which the Christian can initiate himself into 'seeing things from God's point of view', living the experience that St John calls 'remaining in Christ', 'remaining in love' with the variant 'remaining in the love of the Father', 'remaining in the word' etc.[11]

The apprenticeship has received various descriptions throughout the history of spirituality; it has been called the way of humility by Cassian, the way of moderation by the Greek Fathers, the way of constant prayer supported by the signs of inner consolation by St Ignatius of Loyola, or the way of immersion in the word of God.[12]

2. The Christian should not fear to let himself be freely carried away by the Spirit, who in free and unlooked-for ways, will suggest unsuspected roads to him. This spiritual impulse does not generally exclude but rather presupposes the exercise of prudential judgment on the various factors at work, leading to a first 'natural' discernment in order to elucidate if what moves the subject proceeds from 'ambition, desire for gain or *libido*' (Pierre d'Ailly), or whether it comes from the truth and the love of God.

This distinction aims at: in the first place, appreciating what are known as 'double motivations' [13] which tend to mask perhaps basically self-interested or egocentric intentions under a cloak of altruism; in the second place, establishing a correct order in the overall process of discernment, given that prudential discernment is taken as the base but left open to the free impulse—whether antecedent, concomitant or later—of the Spirit.

3. There is a real dialectical involvement between prudential judgment and the movement of the Spirit which inspires in 'counsel' and decision.

Prudent judgment acts as a regulating 'measure' on the way of spiritual freedom, verifying that progress along the way produces no harm either to the subject [14] or to third parties. On the other hand, and this is the most important aspect, the Spirit impels us and helps us to find contact with the reality of the world by leading us—as though by a short cut—to know 'what is in the heart of man', by clarifying the texture of human inter-relationships; and allows us, if we are attentive to the 'signs of the times', to read the meaning of history. The Spirit places us in the context of reality seen from the viewpoint of the benevolent and saving love of God. It would seem, however, that contemplative and humble prayer alone enables man to achieve this view of reality which is a blessing in itself!

THE PROBLEM OF CERTAINTY IN DISCERNMENT

Prudent or spiritual discretion is not too easy since it includes the element of uncertainty proper to all processes of choice. These in fact always refer to the particular contingent reality represented by human action.[15] This means that the matter on which discernment acts can never offer the same degree of certainty as that provided by first principles or evident conclusions. Where discernment is concerned, principles and conclusions are measured by a judgment of practical value referring to these uncertain variables represented by human actions in their particularity. This is a summary of what Thomas Aquinas noted with his usual acumen.[16]

The problem of certainty in discernment has a very large influence on the question of who should discern. In our Western mentality, which is not only rational, but has a tendency to rationalism,[17] the uncertainty proper to discernment has proved both a cross and a stimulus to seek supports offering certainty in decision and choice. Fear of uncertainty has played its part in the excesses produced in one way or another: sometimes the blind obedience in which the person directed acts *'tamquam cadaver'* [18] has been offered as a supreme security; at other times, fear of the responsibility, of *'diákrisis'*, has led to desire for personal surrender to a decision-making community. Finally, when the excess has pulled in the opposite direction, fear of the risk implied by obedience or of the weight of the community or of the doctrinal constants that mark out the boundaries of the ecclesial communion, have provoked exaltation of the individual judgment. This is not a matter of praising uncertainty for its own sake, but one has to accept that discernment, even when it does not take the form of 'the conclusion of an operative syllogism' [19] which Thomas Aquinas saw it as doing, can take the form of a serious spiritual intuition which, in its turn, can be guided by experience of life. Here, certainty is not empirical evidence nor that evidence by which mathematical conclusions are deduced, nor is it the subjective certainty of the fanatic. It is the certainty of proceeding along the right way of certain hope; a procedure that can always be perfected, is always open to dialogue—since it supposes dialogue with the community and within the framework of the ecclesial communion—and always open to the supreme measure which is the mode of being and acting of the Lord Jesus. Rather than subjective 'security', discernment offers the more interesting way of acting in the way of the Lord in confident and humble openness of mind.

DISCERNMENT AND OBEDIENCE

For those who tend to assimilate discernment to obedience, the Superior is the person who discerns. How has this change of key come about—representing as it does a slide from the level of knowledge (discretion) to the level of surrendering one's will to that of the Superior (obedience)?

(a) In the first place this is a result of the earlier problem of certainty in discernment. Total obedience seeks a drastic remedy in the belief that this 'is never mistaken'.

(b) Over the centuries, a sort of jurisprudence concerning who should discern has grown up. When this criteriology is properly set out, there is usually a balance kept between the two elements of obedience to the Superior and discernment properly so-called. This is true of the famous quatrain by Pierre d'Ailly in which discernment is attributed equally to the Council, the Pope and the Bishop, all in the line of obedience, but also to the *'Doctor bene doctus'* and the *'Discretor spirituum'* in the line of discernment.[20]

The most significant case, however, is that of the Desert Fathers, who never lose the dialectical balance between obedience and discernment. Even 'obedience without discernment' (*a-diakritós*) never appears separated from its reason for being, which is the need of *diákrisis* on the part of the disciple. Supreme obedience can only stem from a free act of supreme discernment: 'obedience deposes discernment through a superabundance of discernment'.[21]

In practice, on the other hand, the dialectical balance has more than once become an alternative negating one or other of the two poles in tension. Spiritual direction is an example of this. St John of the Cross conceived this as a common discernment in order to 'know and do the truth' in which the 'wise, discreet and experienced' Director took the part of a humble witness to the Spirit.[22] On the other hand, some tendencies over the last few years have led to a 'dictated' mode of direction in which the person directed is treated as 'inert matter'. There could be nothing more opportune at the present time than a return to the mentality of St John of the Cross.

THE ROLE OF THE COMMUNITY

The small community is a reference point in the religious life; it is the element that promotes the knowledge and judgment on the world the Christian should possess if he is to bring to the world the values he most loves and hopes for. On the level of decision-making it is not a substitute for personal responsibility but the vital medium in which this arises and develops. The community should encourage, enrich, guide and refrain, but not coerce; it discerns matters of common interest, particularly the mission and conditions for witness to Christ. The community seeks to be both home and school for spiritual apprenticeship in prayer and humility. This is where the Christian learns to look at people with a look that blesses because it cuts through the bitter skin we all possess to discover in others the visage of the poor.

The ecclesial communion is, finally, the field of the revelation of the

Word, related by the magisterium and interpreted as a risky or faithful doctrinal discernment by the theologians; it is the prophetic people inspired by the Spirit. It is the principal subject of communitary discernment: this discernment is then called 'Council'.

Translated by Paul Burns

Notes

1. John XXIII, *Pacem in Terris,* n. 154. See the whole paragraph.
2. Revelation 2:7, 11, 17, 29; 3:6, 13, 22.
3. *Summa Theol.,* I–II, q 65, a 1.
4. See the article in this issue by C. Marti.
5. *Contra Gentiles,* III, 154.
6. 'Oportet igitur ea quae per fidem tenemus, a Deo in nos pervenire' *Contra Gent.,* III, 154, par. 1.
7. G. Bardy, in *Dict. de Spirit.* (Paris, 1957), III, 1251; (II, 222).
8. A. Cabassut, ibid., III, 1318.
9. Migne, *PG,* 65, 425.
10. See Gregory Nazianzen, 'Funeral Elegy for St Basil', 60, 1.
11. Jn. 15: 4–7, 9–10; 1 Jn. 4: 16; also Jn. 8: 31.
12. Luther, *The Freedom of the Christian:* 'He needs nothing more if he possesses the word of God . . . In this he finds joy, peace, light, understanding . . .'
13. On 'the ambivalent attitude of the subject with regard to the object' cf., S. Freud, *Totem and Taboo,* esp. the ch. on 'The taboo and the ambivalence of feelings'.
14. Ignatius of Loyola, *Spiritual Exercises,* First Week, 10th Addition: 'Provided the subject is not corrupted nor any notable sickness follows'.
15. V. *Summa Theol.,* I–II, qq 13–14.
16. In particular, 'In rebus agendis multa incertitudo invenitur: quia actiones sunt circa singularia contingentia; quae propter suam variabilitatem incerta sunt' (I–II, q 14, a 1).
17. J. M. Rovira, 'Condicionaments racionalistes del pensament teologic occidental', in *Analecta sacra Tarraconsensia,* XLI (1969), pp. 29–70.
18. *Vitae Patrum,* V, 15, 64; *PL* 73, 964d.
19. *Summa Theol.,* I–II, q 13, a 3.
20. P. D'Ailly, *De examinatione,* v. *Dict. de Spirit.,* III, 1264.
21. Climacus, *Scala Paradisi,* 4; *PG* 88, 680; I. Hausherr, *Direction spirituelle en Orient autrefois,* (Rome, 1955).
22. St John of the Cross, *Ascent,* II, 22; *Flame* III, 20, 43, 46.

PART IV

Bulletins

Yves Congar

Archbishop Lefebvre, Champion of 'Tradition'? Some Necessary Clarifications

ARCHBISHOP Lefebvre has abundantly made his views known.[1] One owes it to him to acknowledge that he has not varied what he has to say, and that his thought is simple. Let us first listen to him.

'We adhere, with all our heart and all our soul to Catholic Rome, guardian of the Catholic faith and of the traditions that are necessary for the upholding of that faith, to Rome the eternal, mistress of wisdom and of truth. On the other hand, we refuse, as we always have refused, to follow the Rome of neo-Modernist and neo-Protestant tendencies, which was clearly manifested during the second Vatican Council, and after the council in all the reforms that have flowed from it . . . . No authority, even the most elevated in the hierarchy, can constrain us to abandon or to water down our Catholic faith as it has been clearly expressed and professed by the Magisterium of the Church for nineteen centuries' (Declaration of 21 November 1974: E270).

'I will uphold' (N 16). 'Fight in order to *uphold tradition*' (E289).

'We must hold fast to the preconciliar positions, and not be afraid to appear to be acting in disobedience to the Church when we are carrying on a tradition that is two thousand years old. What should be the criterion of the ordinary magisterium for knowing whether or not it is infallible? The answer is, fidelity to tradition in its entirety' (E170).

'If Your Holiness obliges us to make a crucial choice between yourself and your predecessors, you will oblige us to opt for your predecessors, in whom is found the Church which has lived through the ages from the magisterium and the apostolic tradition, for we do not wish to become either heretics or schismatics, but only to remain faithful members of the age-old Roman Catholic Church' (audience of 11 November 1976)—on the 'age-old Church' and the 'age-old magisterium' see also E271, A9, C12, CP245. 'The Mass of Pius V is the Mass of twenty centuries. It is the traditional Mass' (CP245).

'Tradition, for me, is the magisterium of the Church, infallible for twenty centuries' (CP245). 'Tradition being, according to the teaching of the Church, Christian doctrine defined for all time by the solemn Magisterium of the Church, it is characterized by an immutability which compels the assent of faith, not only of the present generation but of future generations as well . . . Now, how is one to reconcile the affirmations made in the declaration on religious liberty with the teaching of tradition? How is one to reconcile the liturgical reforms with the teaching of the Council of Trent and with tradition? How reconcile the ecumenical movement with the teaching of the Church and canon law concerning the Church's relations with heretics, schismatics, atheists, unbelievers and public sinners?' [2]

A practical conclusion is to be drawn from these convictions: 'This house (Ecône) has resolutely decided to opt for membership of the age-old Church and refuses to belong to the reformed and liberal Church' (E314, N232). Disobedience to the false in order to be faithful to the true. From this moment on 'it is we who will continue the Church' (C16); 'we are in the truth because one cannot be outside the truth when one continues what has been done for two thousand years' (C17). 'We are not in schism, we are the continuers of the Catholic Church; it is those who introduce innovations who have gone into schism; we are carrying on the tradition' (CP223, 247; cf N15). 'We are ready to follow the instructions of the pope. But when he does not follow the instructions of the 262 popes who have gone before him, we cannot follow his'. [3]

POSITIVE ASPECTS OF THIS ATTITUDE

We will recognize, first of all, not only the seriousness of these observations, but also the element of truth contained within them. That which is true is in fact definitively true—and this applies to the trinitarian, christological, eucharistic and ecclesiological dogma. This does not imply either that the dogmas defined in the course of history express the *entire* truth as far as their object is concerned, or that they present the *best* formulation of it, but it does imply a need to respect them. We will even say that many texts of the most reliable authorities proclaim that if a bishop, or a pope even, were to say something contrary to a truth of faith, one should not listen to him, on the contrary, one should admonish him.[4] It is obvious that an accusation of this nature is so grave that it must be most rigorously precise. And so, I ask: what *dogma* have Vatican II, Paul VI and the instructions issued by them denied or called in question? None! Indeed, when theologians or priests have questioned points of doctrine, the Holy Father, the bishops, and in the event myself, denounced and took issue with them. So, why not carry on this fight for the faith together?

We should note yet another positive element. Archbishop Lefebvre returns unwearyingly to the question of the mass and the 'priesthood'. It is a point on which he meets with the agreement of a large number of Catholics. Many, in fact, who would not follow him into schism, nevertheless say: he is right. I personally regret that permission has not been given for the so-called mass of St Pius V to be celebrated alongside that, so-called, of Paul VI. On the one hand, this would have demonstrated that the eucharistic faith had in no way changed (but the Roman canon remains as eucharistic prayer number one, and when I celebrate it thus, on occasion in Latin, what distinguishes my celebration from that of Archbishop Lefebvre?). On the other hand, the deep sensibilities of good Catholics, who find in the celebration of the eucharistic sacrifice the sign of their Catholic identity, would have been better respected. This point is very important, very worthy of consideration. Many people feel lost because their expression of Catholic identity has been taken away from them.

Unfortunately, the supporters of Archbishop Lefebvre have accused the new eucharistic rite of prompting a betrayal of the faith of the Church; they have turned celebration of the Mass according to the Missal of St Pius V—which in any case has undergone a certain number of changes since 1576—into an instrument of impassioned combat against the reform of Paul VI: and this makes a peaceful solution virtually impossible. I need not demonstrate here the falsity of the accusations made—that has been done on more than one occasion. Archbishop Lefebvre has, moreover, admitted the validity of the new rite if it is celebrated with the faith and intention of the eucharistic doctrine of the Council of Trent. But he hardens this doctrine, going so far as to employ very questionable terms, unknown to Trent, such as 'to *renew* the sacrifice of the cross' (E279 and elsewhere).

UNACCEPTABLE MISINTERPRETATIONS AND DENIALS

In order to start making the necessary distinctions, one must get down to a critical appraisal of the positions adopted by Archbishop Lefebvre. I will make such an appraisal in three paragraphs.

1. Archbishop Lefebvre never mentions the sizeable movements which were a feature of the life of the Church during the decades preceding the council: movements without which the council would not have been what it was, for, in so far as what they represented was valid, they there received the seal of approval of the highest authority. The liturgical movement was a century old, and its pastoral expansion had been going on for some sixty years. It was based on work of indisputable value. It made it possible for the insights of the most deeply rooted tradition to live once more in the Catholic consciousness. The biblical movement had got into its stride, likewise sustained by serious activity and encouraged by Pope Pius XII. The patristic movement, of which Père Henri de Lubac's fine work, *Catholicism,* was, as it were, the harbinger in 1938, was already bearing fruits which were multiplied in the post-conciliar period. If Vatican II marked the end of the Counter-Reform, it also reestablished links with many of the values of the Church of the Fathers, of the east as well as of the west. Its authority in the field of ecumenism derives largely from this fact. A serious ecumenical movement also existed, and there was a growing assumption of responsibility by the laity, alongside the bishops and priests, for apostolic and ecclesial activities . . . All this was to some extent *new*, but in no way did it represent a sudden show of strength. It developed in the course of the historical life of the Church, it has continued to develop since the council, and it will go on developing in the future. It is all part of this historical life of the Church.

2. Now, I diagnose in Archbishop Lefebvre a certain rejection of the new acquisitions of this historical life, a rejection of the 'modern world', and even a denial that there are *new* problems calling for *new* responses. 'All the essential questions concerned with mankind have always found their solution, since the beginning of the world and above all, of our Lord Jesus Christ' (A83). 'Those who demand of the Church answers to those questions are, I fear, looking in fact for answers already given by the Church, but which they refuse to accept . . . These excellent people are "the modern world"! They find and invent a host of "questions" for one purpose only: that the Church should today contradict her traditional teaching' (A84). The last two quotations come from a criticism, made in 1964, of the schema on the Church in the modern world. It is worth noting that it was that text and the text *Nostra aetate* (In our age), on the non-Christian religions, that Archbishop Lefebvre refused to sign. Both relate to the present moment, involving an element of acceptance of new situations of facts. One could make a similar observation on the subject of researches in the field of catechesis (a term Archbishop Lefebvre rejects!) and of the Roman Synod of 1977. For Archbishop Lefebvre the 'modern' is to be

rejected as such; he slips fairly often from 'modern' to 'modernist' (cf E79, C5).

This is because what is 'modern' is infested with 'liberalism'—I will come back to the content of this term. Thus, in what he describes as the age-old tradition, the age-old Magisterium, Archbishop Lefebvre refers to the following as having completed the 'doctrine of Trent': the bull *Auctorem fidei* of Pius VI against Pistoia, *Mirari vos* of Gregory XVI against Lamennais, *Quanta cura* and the Syllabus of Pius IX, *Immortale Dei* of Leo XIII 'condemning the new law', the *Acts* of St Pius X against *Le Sillon* and Modernism, *Divini Redemptoris* of Pius XI against Communism and finally *Humani Generis* of Pius XII (E317–318). All these are documents *contra:* against errors, against tendencies, against 'liberalism'.

One cannot fail to note a political undercurrent in these very clearly defined positions. Archbishop Lefebvre rejects the charge that he has been a follower of Maurras or of the Action Française. But (1) Archbishop Lefebvre has a paternalistic notion of authority, 'the formal cause of society' (E84)—I say this without denying what he rightly affirms, that there is no fraternity without paternity; (2) he has given as models of the Catholic Church the Spain of Franco or the Portugal of Salazar (E101), Argentina (CP217) and the Chile of Pinochet (CP246); (3) finally, all the evil comes, in his view, from the French Revolution, with its motto of 'Liberty, Equality, Fraternity'—'Satan invented these key words, which have allowed all sorts of modern and modernist words to seep into the council: liberty has come in through religious liberty or the liberty of the religions; equality through collegiality, which has introduced the principles of democratic egalitarianism into the Church; and finally fraternity, through the ecumenism which embraces all heresies and errors and holds out its hand to all the enemies of the Church' (C5; cf E196, 259, 288, Letter to Paul VI of 17 July 1976).

3. Archbishop Lefebvre treats all the 'condemnations' contained in the documents to which he refers as absolute, as if it were a question of dogmatic judgments reproving heresies. He does not distinguish, as would any historian, between a rejection of formal theological errors and the element of historical contingency appreciated by the pastoral authority, and eventually even recognized in the policy of churchmen. He lumps together in the same condemnation all that displeases him in the modern movements, ecumenism (E111) and the so-called Charismatic Renewal (E264, 297; N146). The quintessence of heresy as far as he is concerned is liberalism—that is to say the reaching of an understanding with the Reform, with the Revolution (E100, 288), total freedom, leaving everything to conscience (E259) 'liberating man from

every constraint that he does not himself will or accept' (E315). The conciliar declaration on religious liberty is likened, in spite of what it expressly says, to 'the religious indifferentism condemned by the doctrine and the teaching authority of the Church' (C27).

If the historical aspect of the pastoral magisterium, if the distinctions that need to be made where modern movements are concerned, so elude Archbishop Lefebvre, it is because his mind is absorbed with eternist formulations.[5] 'The truth has an eternal character' (C31, 34), for God is immutable (ibid.), and Jesus Christ is yesterday, today and the same forever (C12, 31). The facts mentioned are incontestable in themselves, but they do not preclude the historicity of *our* perception and of *our* expression of the truth, above all in matters which touch on social realities, movements of ideas, or the activities of states, as is largely the case for the Syllabus of Pius IX. This gives me an opportunity to say how I approach this important document which was appended to the encyclical *Quanta Cura* (8 December 1864).

THE SYLLABUS

1. These are important documents: Pius IX and Leo XIII have declared them to be so. They contain within them doctrinal pronouncements that we will have to respect, even if in a completely different historical, social and cultural context.

2. In spite of Vacant, whose maximizing interpretation of the ordinary magisterium of the pope no one supports,[6] one cannot characterize *Quanta cura* or the Syllabus as infallible teaching. This is proved (a) by the fact that such infallibility is denied by Mgr Fesset, who was secretary to the first Vatican Council and whose book received the approbation of Pius IX;[7] and (b) by the fact that the document was so definitely not considered to be infallible teaching that the most ardent supporters of the papal magisterium wanted its teaching to be proclaimed by the council.[8] Others feared that this would be done.

3. *Quanta cura* cannot be rightly understood except within the philosophico-political and social context of the time. This is even truer of the Syllabus, which refers to various pontifical interventions, consistorial allocutions in many cases, concerned with the politico-religious situations in various countries (Mexico; Europe; above all and decisively Italy.[9] In many regions a levelling type of rule was rampant, drawing its inspiration from the jurists or the philosophers of the eighteenth century and harmful to the *libertas Ecclesiae* and the authority of the see of Rome. The question of the temporal power of the Holy See was also decisive. To take the pronouncents, the words themselves, out of their historical context is to lay oneself open to the

risk of giving them an absolute meaning and significance which go beyond and, in so doing, betray their truth. This is particularly true of the word 'liberalism'. In reality, it masked a rationalism applied by the powers in the State in an antireligious policy.[10] It has therefore been challenged, as well as by Pius IX or Leo XIII, by a Newman (who pronounced the toast to conscience!) and by the social Catholics studied by E. Poulat.[11]

4. Pius IX and Leo XIII still spoke from within the perspective of 'Christianity', that is to say from a situation in which the temporal powers were regarded as subject to the norms promulgated by the Church, which they took as the basis of the laws of their own government. Now in such a situation, permanent principles stemming from the divine mission of the Church are mixed with the historical conditions emerging from the (more or less) public law acknowledged, precisely, in the ages of 'Christendom'. The popes themselves have recognized this, and not only Paul VI, but Pius XII and, in part at least, Pius IX.[12] In the same way, the popes, from Leo XIII to Pius XI, Pius XII and above all the John XXIII of *Pacem in terris,* have ever more clearly and resolutely vindicated the dignity of the human person against restrictive regimes or practices, in such a way that the conciliar document *Dignitatis humanae personae* forms part of a continuous severance.[13] The popes before Vatican II followed the evolution of modern society, which is something Archbishop Lefebvre unfortunately refuses to do.

5. This does not mean that the Church adopts the principles of the rationalist liberalism or the secularism that she has condemned and that Vatican II has likewise criticized.[14] What it does mean is that in the earlier teachings of the magisterium there exists a basic substratum, an essential corpus of principles which we should always respect, but which were in the past expressed in an historical context that is no longer ours and which today we should respect *in another way.* I have no space here to develop this point, but I would like to illustrate it with three examples: (a) the documents of Pius IX and Leo XIII against rationalist liberalism. (b) The deceptively obvious principle, 'outside the Church no salvation' and the contemporary documents, whether of the Holy Office in the Feeney affair or of Vatican II.[15] (c) The passage in twenty or thirty years from *Mortalium Animos* (6 January 1928) to the instruction *Ecclesia Catholica* of December 1949 and the conciliar decree on ecumenism.[16] There exists, in fact, a continuity of essential principles, a development, a new and different expression of principles and their aim in a new and different historical context.

These considerations do not constitute a digression. They bring us to the core of those distinctions which relate to the notion of tradition.

THE TRUE NOTION OF TRADITION. DISTINCTIONS

Tradition is a vast reality. I have devoted a number of studies to it.[17] It means, for the Church, confronting its present and its future in the light of its past roots. In this sense, I could take up the formula of Archbishop Lefebvre himself: 'It is because our faith is the faith of the past that it is also the faith of the future' (C17, 34). Tradition is, in fact, the presence of a principle to its entire history. But more precisely, there exist at one and the same time the identity of the principle and the historical reality of situations, forms and expressions. This is so for the two following reasons: (1) Tradition is not only transmission but also reception. Nothing would be effectively transmitted were it not also received. Whence the need to translate and adapt. This is what has been done in particular where it is a matter of institution—liturgy, ministries, papacy. These things have *one* history! (2) Tradition is a great river which, since its source in revelation and the Gospel, has flowed through many countries and many centuries. The river has thus received from various tributaries, which have mingled their contribution with that of the source. There have been the questions posed in the course of time and in different climates by the different world movements or by heresies. There have also been the contributions of cultures, geniuses and saints, of the whole life of the People of God. Tradition, such as it has come down to us, is made up of all that, so that it is possible to distinguish within it the absolute quality of the principle, gradually developed or clarified, and the historical forms associated with different ages, the more or less changing contexts. Let us listen at this point to three of the most recent Roman pontiffs:

'Tradition is something very different from simple attachment to a past that has disappeared: it is quite the opposite of a reaction that distrusts all healthy progress . . . The word "progress" indicates simply the fact of the march forward. "Tradition" still signifies a march forward, but a continuous march, which unfolds at the same time with strength and tranquillity, according to the laws of life'.[18]

'It is above all necessary that the Church should not lose contact with the sacred heritage of truth received from the fathers, but at the same time she must also keep her eye on the present, on the new conditions and forms of life introduced in the modern world, which have opened up new avenues for the Catholic apostolate . . . The substance of the ancient doctrine contained in the *deposit of faith* is one thing, the way in which it is formulated is another . . .' [19]

'Tradition is not a fossilized or dead entity, a reality in some way static, which at a given moment in history blocks the life of that active organism which is the Church, that is to say, the mystical body of Christ. It is for the Pope and for the ecumenical councils to make a judgment, in order to discern what in the traditions of the Church it is not possible to renounce without being unfaithful to the Lord and the Holy Spirit—the deposit of faith—and what on the contrary can and must be brought up to date, in order to facilitate prayer and the mission of the Church throughout the variety of times and places, to translate the divine message more effectively into the language of today and to communicate it better, without undue compromise. Basically, you listen to yourself and those who follow you. You stop at a particular moment in the life of the Church, and in so doing you refuse to adhere to the living Church, which is the age-old Church . . .' [20]

Here then are the principles for clarification that were called for. This clarification relates to the distinction between the one principle and its historical forms. One misses it when, for want of information and historical sense, one adopts a fixist, eternist position; when, having chosen one's poles of reference from among those opposed to the corrupt novelties of the modern world, one makes an absolute of the way in which they are expressed, confusing the relative of history and the absolute of faith. One can call this 'dogmatism' or 'ideology', or else, in medical terms, paranoia. It is sad that a fidelity that is obviously so sincere and in itself praiseworthy, can be so mistaken in its application! The Church has need of it, provided it is exercised in communion with its present life.

Translated by Sarah Fawcett

Notes

1. Abbreviations used:
   E   Archbishop Marcel Lefebvre, *Un évêque parle, Ecrits et allocutions 1963–1975* (Dominique Martin-Morin, 1976).
   A   Archbishop Lefebvre, *J'accuse le Cocile!* (Editions Saint-Gabriel, CH 1920 Martigny, October 1976).
   C   Archbishop Lefebvre, *Le coup de maître de Satan.* Ecône face à la persécution (Saint-Gabriel, 1977).
   P   Minutes of the interview with Cardinals Garrone, Tabera and Wright, 3 March 1975. In R. Gaucher, *Mgr Lefebve combat pour l'Englise* (Paris, 1976, pp. 216–61).
   CP Press conference held by Archbishop Lefebvre on 15 September 1976. In J. A. Chalet, *Monseigneur Lefebre* (Paris, 1976, pp. 233–48—see on pp. 205–26 the text of his discourse in Lille on 23 August 1976).

N   *Non,* interviews of José Hanu with Archbishop Lefebvre (Paris, 1977).

2. Letter of Archbishop Lefebvre to Pope Paul VI, 3 December 1976. In *Documentation Catholique* no. 1715, 6 March 1977, p. 229.

3. Address in New York, 6 November 1977. In *Le Monde,* 9 November 1977, p. 19.

4. I have quoted these texts, in particular those of St Anselm, Gratian and St Thomas Aquinas in *Apostolicité de ministère et apostolicité de doctrine* Festgabe J. Höfer (Freiburg im Breisgau, 1967), pp. 84–111; *Ministères et Communion ecclésiale* (Paris, 1971, pp. 51–94).

5. See 'La Rome eternelle' (E270) and, in a milieu sympathetic to the ideas of Archbishop Lefebvre, Marquis de la Franquerie, *Charles Maurras, défenseur de l'Eglise et des principes éternels;* M. Mad. Martin, *Le Latin immortel.*

6. J-M. A. Vacant, *Le magistère ordinaire de l'Eglise et ses organes* (Paris-Lyons, 1887), pp. 102ff. Cf. J. Bellamy, *Le théologie catholique au XIX siècle* (Paris, 1904), pp. 239ff.

7. Mgr Fessler, *La vraie et la fausse infaillabilité* (French translation, Paris 1873), pp. 8ff, 132ff.

8. Thus the famous article in *Civiltà Cattolica,* 6 February 1869. It was the wish of one Rodrigo Guste in the preparatory commission. See also that which Mgr Preppel wrote to Mgr Maret on 20 February 1869. During the council itself, the idea was mentioned again, but the majority, including Pius IX himself considered the matter inopportune. See among others R. Aubert, *Vatican I* (*coll. Les Conciles oecuméniques*) (Paris, 1964), pp. 71, 75, passim.

9. On this subject see E. Ollivier, *L'Eglise et l' Etat au concile du Vatican,* second edition, vol. I, pp. 342–55; R. Aubert, *Le Pontificat de Pie IX.* (Paris, 1951); 'L'enseignements du Magistere ecclesiastique aux XIXe siècle sur le liberalism', in *Tolérance et Communauté humaine* (Brussels, 1952), pp. 75–103.

10. 'In France, as in Belgium, throughout the nineteenth century, the label ''liberal'' continued to feed in the first instance the worst anticlerical and even antireligious fanaticism': J. Lecler, 'Les controverses sur l'Eglise et l'Etat au temps de la restauration (1815–1830)', in *L'Ecclésiologie au XIXe siècle* (Paris 1960), p. 305, n. 23; ibid, 'La papauté moderne et la liberté de conscience', in *Etudes,* 249 (1946), pp. 298ff.

11. E. Poulat, *Eglise contre Bourgeoisie. Introduction au devenir du Catholicisme actuel* (Brussels, 1977).

12. *Reférences dans notre Eglise catholique et France moderne* (Paris, 1978), p. 265, n. 7.

13. See the articles of R. Aubert, E. Borne, M.-D. Chenu in *Essais sur la liberté religieuse* (Recherches et Débats no. 50, March 1965); J. C. Murray, 'Vers une intelligence du développement de la doctrine de l'Eglise sur la liberté religieuse', in Vatican II and 'La liberté religieuse', *Unam Sanctam* 60 (Paris, 1967), pp. 111–47.

14. The decree *Apostolicam actuositatem,* no. 7.

15. Explanations and references in my article of 1956 which appeared in *Catholicisme,* vol. V, pp. 948–56 and was taken up again in *Sainte Eglise,* Paris 1963, pp. 417–32; Vatican II, *Lumen Gentium,* 16, and *Ad Gentes,* 7.

16. See the lecture I wrote for the fiftieth anniversary of Lausanne, 'Cinquante années de recherche de l'unité' (Lausanne, 1977); *Cinquante ans de Foi et Constitution* (Geneva, 1977), pp. 20–34; and in *Istina* 23 (1978).

17. *La Tradition et les traditions*, I. *Essai historique*, II. *Essai théologique* (Paris, 1960, 1963); *La Tradition et la vie de l'Eglise* (Paris, 1963); *Tradition in Theology: A Symposium on Tradition* (*The Great Ideas Today*, 1974: *Encyclopaedia Britannica*), cols. 4–20.

18. Pius XII, discourse to the Roman nobility, 19 January 1944.

19. John XXIII, discourse at the opening of the council, 11 October 1962.

20. Paul VI, letter of 11 October 1976 to Archbishop Lefebvre, published in French in the *Osservatore Romano*, 10 December 1976.

Casimir Marti

Discernment and Life Revision

THE expression 'life revision' was first used in the thirties in JOC circles. Together with other formulae such as 'inquest-campaign', 'search for the Gospel', 'team work',[1] it was a semantic reflection of an important innovation in modes of behaviour current in the Catholic Church, and furthermore, a broadening of what is usually called Christian contemplation.

Indeed, under the JOC's influence, a more realistic consideration was given to the problems of living, and in particular to the problems of the world of work, which had begun with Christian democracy[2] and Christian trade unionism, to politics and the workers' struggle, and with the help of modernism and biblical criticism, to the field of theological reflection. The Catholic workers' initiative in the face of the problems of the working class, led by the JOC, can be considered as the creator of a type of behavior which was quite new and different from the usual model of Christian action in the Church at the time.

The dominant model in the Catholic world was imposed by the Church with rigorous measures to preserve it from the influence of the attitude and customs prevalent outside the Church, and by group discipline maintained by cultic and moral practices. These were the ordinary means used by the Church to hold the modern world which had escaped its tutelage at bay, and to try to regain its control over civil society which it had held in previous centuries.

All attempts by Catholics to make contact with the reality of the modern world had to confront the distrust and even the condemnations of the Catholic hierarchy, who could count on the support of the mass of the faithful. The seriousness of the situation and the importance of these attempts can be realized more fully if we do not forget the fact that their protagonists usually did not propose purely and simply to abandon the desire that the Church should regain the influence it had had over society in previous centuries, but rather they wanted to re-establish this influence in other ways than that of offended and contemptuous withdrawal from the world.

For the JOC and then for other such movements, life revision in this context came to mean an instrument for a triple encounter: encounter with the reality of daily life, including that which escaped the Church's tutelage; encounter of the Christian subject with himself without the inhibitions of a siege mentality imposed by the Church; encounter with the word of God, considered in new situations, or situations experienced as new, which made new areas of life open to salvation, and offered fresh motives for thanksgiving and adoration.

In this triple encounter with the reality of daily life, the self, and the Word of God, various forms of discernment were used which I shall analyze.

ENCOUNTER WITH REALITY

Life revision took as its starting point the 'facts of life'. It tried to think about and analyze the facts experienced by Christians in real life.

The facts of life experienced by simple Christians—like the young people militant in the JOC and other similar movements—were always the events of ordinary life. In fact they were hardly ever concerned with the fate of the world, and the psychological quality of the operation would be dubious if the Christian experiencing these facts and trying to think about them and analyze them, felt obliged to give them a transcendental significance which they did not really have.

This analysis of ordinary daily life could reach varying depths. It could be a simple description of experienced fact. Or it could go into the causes and consequences of it. Or it could study the structural dynamism (economic, political, psychological) which are involved in the occurrence of this fact and condition it.

Of course the exercise of faith does not require as a *sine qua non* a grasp of reality which attains the highest degree of rigour. But the shallower analysis can always go deeper, and the person moved by faith is not thereby given a license to refuse an even deepening perception of reality; indeed he is impelled towards this growing perception by the very dynamism of the call to faith, which pierces all human reality 'to the marrow' (cf. Heb. 4: 12–13).

In all three cases (the simple description of the experienced fact, the analysis of causes and consequences—linear analysis—or perception of structural factors—dialectical analysis), a Christian is driven in the name of his life of faith to take on reality.

From the point of view of the presence of the Church in the modern world, accepting real facts means beginning to overcome the wary and hostile attitude towards the modern world which largely characterized the Church during the previous century and the first decades of this one. In this attempt to grasp reality, Christians who were thrown together with all kinds of people during the Second World War—in the trenches, in the resistance, in the Nazi concentration camps—were made to realize the Church's alienation from the true situation of their contemporaries and obliged to abandon their attitude of competitive hostility to the forces inspired by Socialism.

Congar recalls the years 1925–40 as a stage of growing awareness, during which the boys and girls in the Catholic Action movements brought to priests, who were isolated from the world through their education, a sense of their own dignity and their cultural functions, data about the religious state, reading matter and leisure activities of the alienated masses. And then came the Second World War which violently removed the established barriers and made it possible to conceive of the religious reality of the people as a true 'state of mission'.[3]

The polemics against Socialism also engaged in by the JOC in its early years [4] diminished in the atmosphere of closeness and collaboration established between Christians and Socialists in the circumstances of the world war.[5]

From another point of view it was very important that the iniative to make Christian sense of reality was taken by movements like the JOC. Because if a few Christians living in the contemporary world merely tried to live their faith in a solid manner, it could not properly be said that it was the whole Church reconciling itself with the world. But from the beginning the JOC attempted a truly ecclesial movement. The support sought by Cardijn from popes and ecclesiastical hierarchy was something very different from an act of opportunism. Objectively it offered the whole Church the possibility, in recognizing the JOC experience as ecclesial, of also recognizing itself in a relationship with the world quite different from that established by Gregory XVI and Pius IX.

In the plan for the practical functioning of 'life revision', experience enables us to formulate the following two warnings. First, because of the usually partial and fragmentary nature of the facts submitted to analysis, the person offering them is not usually fully reflected in them. However, partial expressions of a person are not negligible merely because they are partial. Because the whole person is present, more or less fully, in every situation experienced.

Second, a particular fact experienced by a single member of a given group may not have been experienced by the other members. Further-more, part of the meeting may forcibly be devoted to the exploration of what similar situations to that of the fact under examination have been experienced by each member of the group. However if the other mem-bers take the fact under analysis and the person who has experienced it seriously, they may already feel involved. Moreover, probably if the analysis of the fact is extended to its causes and consequences, and the structural factors involved, it will be more likely that all the members of the group feel included through their own human and Christian experience.

ENCOUNTER OF THE SUBJECT WITH HIMSELF

Life revision does not only try to grasp and analyze experienced facts objectively. Another important part is the expression of the reac-tions of the person who experienced it to the fact. These feelings may be more or less coherent or contradictory; perception of the real pos-sibilities of action; experience of the limits of one's own capacity to deal with problems, or even the capacity of team work; grasping the level of awareness of one's conditioning by external structures—ethical judgments, and so on.

This attention paid to the subjects' reaction gave rise to the criticism that life revision was merely an off-shoot of personalist philosophy and was unaware of the structural factors which objectively condition ac-tion and the life itself of subjects.

There is no need to emphasize that paying attention to subjective reactions could never be a substitute for the objective consideration of facts and their dynamism. In life revision this attention paid to the subject is merely a step taken before the analysis of facts objectively.

Furthermore examining subjective reaction to facts acted as a counter-weight to the idealistic-voluntarist mechanisms flourishing in the Church, a Church which in spite of having a siege mentality to the modern world, still claimed to represent the whole world and all men in conformity with the individual and social ethical models derived from its doctrines.

The example of class struggle, typical of industrial society, gives an indication of the way in which these idealist-voluntarist mechanisms function, and enables us to appreciate the contribution of life revision to Christian behaviour. The Christian ideal of living together in har-mony is contained in the precept to love one another. In the name of this ideal the Church repeatedly condemned the class struggle, and for many decades simply refused to accept it as a fact. A faithful Christian thus indoctrinated tended to evade reality, sometimes in very subtle ways, because he could not naturally incorporate into his view of things a factor as important as the class struggle. Thus when a Christian fought for justice in the workers' struggle, he tended to see the motives and objectives of this fight in terms derived from an idealist doctrine. In Christian action recourse to ideology and ethical voluntarism had greater weight than a correct analysis of reality.

In life revision, consideration of subjective reactions, invited a Christian to pay attention to his real feelings and thus overcome a simplistic vision of himself in which what really mattered was the conformity or nonconformity of his actions to a model set up *a priori*. In the example of the class struggle, a Christian could cut short evasive recourse to the prevalent idealist-voluntarist mechanisms abovementioned, and discover himself firmly inserted in a contradictory world, which aroused contradictory feelings, which there was no easy way to reconcile.

ENCOUNTER WITH THE WORD OF GOD

Confrontation with the word of God was a crucial point in the process of life revision. Beginning with the analysis of fact, then going on to the exploration of the subject's reaction, was a way of deepening the life of faith based on reality.

When this point was reached in life revision, discernment could no longer be confined to analysis or introspection. For a Christian to enter into relationship with God, it was not enough to examine rigorously the reality in which he lived or his own feelings about it. Analysis and introspection could at best lead to an experience of emptiness and a theist ideology.

But to practice his faith, a Christian approaches the person of Jesus. Jesus appears in our world as a witness to an experience of a single God. Jesus' judgment of reality is God's judgment. In his human experience, Jesus continually encountered the reality of God his Father. In referring to Jesus a Christian recognizes the fulness of human experience of God, the fulness of God's gifts to mankind. In Jesus God realized his plans for our hope. In Jesus' human life, lived by him as God's Son, and in his everlasting life with God after he had conquered death, a Christian discerns and contemplates one by one God's ancient promises which he fulfilled in Jesus and is still fulfilling in human beings throughout history till the end of time.

In the analysis a Christian makes of the reality in which he lives, reference to Jesus neither upsets his data gained by observation, verified and expressed with the means offered by the culture of his time, nor alters the personal possibilities of each individual. Reference to

Jesus is a global 'judgment' of the world, just as Jesus' own life on earth was a 'judgment' of the world. By the mere fact of his presence in the world, Jesus pointed continually to the Father and showed up the inconsistent and 'condemned' nature of all that did not submit to him through faith (cf. Jn. 3:16–21 and 5:24). By referring to Jesus a Christian exercises this 'judgment' of the world.

A Christian who becomes aware of his own reactions and feelings with the means of self-observation at his disposal, takes his own human experience and compares it with the human experience of Jesus, to see whether there are similarities between fundamental lines or fragmentary details characterizing the human experience of a Christian and the lines and details in the life of Jesus. When similarities are found this enables the Christian to hope steadfastly that the Father also loves him, that he is also God's son, and the divine gifts which Jesus experienced and still experiences as his own, also belong to a Christian. Thus discernment of the Word of God leads a Christian to find himself in the radical relationship with the Father he shares with Jesus.

Of course there is no need for the comparison between a Christian's experience and Jesus' experience to be made in an ingenuous way, as the preceding paragraph might suggest, or as, for example, the author of the *Imitation of Christ* proposes. The Christian who has at his disposal the instruments of historical and textual criticism of scripture will be aware of the deep solid tradition in which this practice of searching the Scriptures to find Jesus is rooted and preserved by the Church in its communal experience. The early Christian communities, which were subject to persecution and were undergoing the drama of the break with the synagogue and its customs, suffering problems of internal divisions, and so on, reconstructed the figure of Jesus in the aspects that could be of most help to them to consolidate their communities and practise their faith (cf. Jn. 21.31.). All the New Testament books reflect this exercise of religious memory by the community, in faith and hope. And this discernment of the word of God made flesh, to feed faith and hope, has always been practiced by the Church gathered together in the eucharist, with its gaze fixed on Jesus' return.

The practice of life revision, and in general the spiritual experience of Christians in every age, tends to seek a moralizing extrapolation of a reading of the Gospel. This voluntarist and ethical bias in recourse to the Gospel, in the case of life revision must be complemented by the need—felt very strongly in the context of a Church globally dissociated and inhibited from the tasks of the class struggle and political life—to take responsibility for real life and initiative in it. With ecclesial life in the state it is, it is understandable that people should want to seek in the reading of the Gospel, effective guidance for action.

There was a similar tendency to moralizing reductionism in Spain and elsewhere, in some of the handbooks designed for the use of those who practiced life revision. They were like dictionaries of gospel references on points of Christian behaviour: commitment, poverty, sincerity, hypocrisy, suffering, brotherly love, energy, solidarity, and so on.

In Franco's Spain this moralist reading of the Gospel and of papal doctrine helped to show up the contradiction in a regime which professed itself Catholic and did not believe in accordance with the requirements of the Catholic criteria of justice and freedom.

These handbooks made a summary and functional use of the gospels suggesting the necessity to separate Christian faith from the Franco dictatorship supported by official Catholicism. This led to the reading of the gospels being confined to the extraction of certain moral maxims encouraging action in so far as these ethical criteria still retained a socio-cultural vigour. But one of the results of this purely moral use of the gospel was that its specific message was often disregarded or left implicit: the gospel is the good news of God come to us in Christ.

Life revision whose potentialities as an exercise in discernment I have discussed in its three separate stages, has an internal dynamism we have only suggested in passing, and which I now turn to to conclude. Life revision, like nearly all Christian experience in the Church, is concerned with contemplating God's gifts to us in Christ, and preparing to recognize them as alive and active here and now, in this world, in particular people living now. Those who are called to share God's gifts in Christ are not beings living in the clouds; they have feet, hands, head and heart in this world. Understanding as precisely and deeply as possible the reality of the world about us—discernment of facts—and the situation, attitudes and reactions of the people living in this world—discernment of the subject—make possible a new understanding of the Word of God—discernment of the gospel—and a new mind to receive the gifts God offers. Contemplation of the gifts of God in Christ and receptivity to them, are a new inspiration to action. In order to keep his sonship to the Father, a Christian is called to choose between different possibilities of action which are offered to him in every situation in life. Thus we have the dialectical movement between action and contemplation.

This exercise in analysis and contemplation, starting from action and returning to it, was used by the JOC in its efforts to evangelize the workers. Later the life revision method was adopted by other groups to evangelize other sectors alienated from the Church. In fact although the practice of life revision, with all its requirements of rigour, is still continued as a method by special groups, its result has gone beyond these and had an effect on many Christian communities. The Sunday eucharist, by means of homilies, participation of the faithful in the commentary on the word of God, and the prayers of the people, explicitly incorporates experience of real life into the contemplation of scripture and the eucharistic celebration itself. Thus what began as an exercise practiced by a more aware minority of Christians is becoming the common property of all believers.

Translated by Dinah Livingstone

Notes

1. Marguerite Fievrez, Jacques Meert, Roger Aubert, *La vida de un pionero: Cardijn* (Barcelona 1970), p. 159.

2. On Christian democracy, modernism and the current driving both movements (rationalization of political life and rationalization of theological reflection), I must mention the excellent book by Maurice Montuclard, *Conscience réligieuse et democratie* (Paris, 1965).

3. Yves Congar, *Vraie et fausse réforme dans l'Eglise* (Paris, 1969), pp. 48–50.

4. Loc. cit. in n. 1, p. 116. This constant hostility to Socialism in Catholic social writing in Spain is noted by Juan Joe Castillo in *El sindicalismo amarillo en Espana* (Madrid, 1977).

5. Loc. cit. in n. 1, pp. 186–87. Alfonso Carlos Comin attributes similar results to the contacts between Christians and Marxists in the long period of clandestine struggle against the Franco dictatorship in Spain in *Cristianos en el partido, comunistas en la Iglesia* (Barcelona, 1977), pp. 41–47.

PART V

Conclusion

Fernando Urbina

On Spirit and History

THE HISTORICAL DIALECTIC OF CHRISTIAN ACTION AND THE SPIRIT

THIS article tries to gather together certain previous theses and in the light of another complementary perspective, to reflect on Christian action in its innermost dialectic: that between Spirit and History.[1]

In New Testament times, we find, especially in St Paul, the elements of a possible theory of evangelical action. There is no reference to laws as universal norms. The stress is on 'discernment' (*dokimazein*).[2] This capacity for discernment is theologically based on a Christian's new life, whose active force is the Spirit,[3] which is set against the power of the flesh. The opposing pair, spirit and flesh, were interpreted then in terms of Greek ascetics, which was totally different from Paul's eschatological theory of action.

The Spirit is power, the guiding norm and meaning of Christian action with reference to the fundamental event of Jesus Christ's resurrection, and open to the future of hope. The normative content (not in a legalistic form, but as a measure of value) is given by fundamental reference to the model action of Jesus Christ: love is the absolute content of the law.[4] St Augustine expresses this Pauline ethic in his categorical imperative: 'love and do what you will'. This imperative governs Christian action in a freedom which is a supreme requirement to give and to serve. Thus Christian action is given its foundation, content and meaning: spiritual discernment, the service of love, eschatological hope.

Paul attacks enthusiastic and ecstatic pseudo-interpretations of the

117

Spirit, reminding the Corinthian community that we are still in the time of the cross.[5] In a text which is fundamental to the understanding of the radical meaning to the historical dialectic of the cross (Rom. 8), the solution is said to come after the *parousia:* meanwhile we have the dialectical tension between *elpis* and *upomones,* hope and patience.

The Christian practice of action, based on its reference to the Spirit and the Gospel, and marked by its eschatological tension, could have offered the material for a specifically Christian theory of action in the world. In fact the sphere of this action was still the small community animated by charismata [6] and inserted in the world.

But the indefinite prolongation of historical time (before the *parousia*) led to a relaxing of the eschatological tension and a reinterpretation of Christian action in terms taken from the ethics and ideas of the world outside: first stoic and neo-Platonic ethics, then Aristotelian, and so on. The sphere of action which is the spiritual community was also radically transformed.

After the peace of Constantine, Christian action was no longer referred to the eschatological sphere of the kingdom, but became enclosed within the absolute space claimed by the hierarchical Church. It was no longer a community of the Spirit animated by 'energies and charismata' [7] but increasingly a *corpus christianorum* with a firm juridical structure.

Now there was just one sphere of action: the Church which absorbed and became the ethical and legal basis for all possible Christian action in the world.

The New Testament conception of an eschatological and spiritual community was changed into the idea of a *corpus sacramentale.* The pope, the vicar of Peter in the first place, and ultimately of Christ, 'the possessor of all power' is the head of this body which, reinterprets Paul's metaphor in terms of the ancient political notion of the social body, whose head, the *princeps,* is absolutely dominant. This ideology was confirmed by the neo-Platonic ideas of the pseudo-Denis and the notion of Spirit in the Church was supplanted by that of power, which always descends from above downwards and is concentrated in the head. The pope inherited the Roman conception of *auctoritas* and *potestas.* The *corpus sacramentale* became the even more formidable *Rechtssystem,* or legal system of history. Political power itself constituted by the emperor and the 'second estate' formed by the nobility [8] were merely the secular arm of papal power. This development was confined to the West. In the East it was the other way round: the *Basileus* was the *Caput* or *Rex-Sacerdos.*[9]

This supreme synthesis of the Middle Ages (from Gregory VII to

Innocent III) led to a real papal theocracy,[10] but internal tensions soon arose boding future schisms in Christian conscience and action.

1. Political power fought for its independence, thus creating the initial impetus for a growing secularization culminating in the French Revolution. A breach was made in the unity of the *corpus christianorum* and in Christian consciousness, which the Church could not accept until it officially recognized the autonomy of human action in the world.[11]

But this process began a split in Christian consciousness which Hegel lucidly diagnoses.[12] However his impressive attempt to reconcile faith and secular reason fails; perhaps the root of Hegel's dramatic failure is his mistaken conception of the Spirit. We may well wonder what marvellous possibilities might have remained open if this great genius with all his rigour and honesty had been directed by the Tübingen theological school towards the true notion of the Spirit in the New Testament.

2. A second dramatic cause of dissociation was the inquisitorial rigour of the 'law system', which made the Church expel from its membership the majority of movements which tried to regain the original spiritual and eschatological meaning of action. Even Franciscanism was quickly silenced.[13]

3. And above all there was a split among the 'spirituals' who kept the principle of the spirit alive. Even among them 'discernment' became a professional activity for a master or spiritual director. Spiritual action quitted real life and became enclosed within the micro-universes of the monasteries.

The ethics of real, social, daily action (love, work, economic relations) were explained in the great scholastic treatises by means of the Aristotelian model of action as practical reason. The essential connection between the 'Nichomacean ethics' and politics was broken and politics ceased to be treated scientifically or at most was restricted to 'advice to princes'.[14]

4. The 'supernatural end' which was higher—by means of an absolute court—than the end of human action (in spite of St Thomas's bridge of possible 'transcendence' [15] of *desiderium naturale,* perhaps so close to Kant's transcendence of practical reason [16] introduced a new and complete split in human action thus adding to the *escotomia* or split between body and soul the even more serious split between natural and supernatural, which attacked at its very roots the necessary

unity of action. Today we have realized that it is radically impossible to heal this serious split with the 'naturalist-substantialist' categories in which the paradigm [17] or model of Christian action was contained until Vatican II. The 'supernatural' is merely another 'nature above', like one brick on top of another or two separate substantial things with no real connection between them possible. Perhaps modern historico-existentialist categories of the 'person open to the infinite' in the absolute newness of history could heal this ancient wound.[18] In fact, the Pauline-Augustinian tradition of the subject moved by the Spirit was lost.

Here in the great crisis of the sixteenth and seventeenth centuries, the true 'labour pains' of modernity, we should reinstate Ignatius' brilliant discovery. Ignatius defined the modern concept of the individual vocation, as did Luther from another standpoint. The subject with his individual vocation is restored to the Pauline-Augustinian tradition of action directed by the discernment of the Spirit, and projected onto the eschatological horizon of God's plan, under the still medieval image of the knight and his earthly king, seeing that St Ignatius, like Luther, still had one foot in the Middle Ages and the other in modern times. Thus Christian action no longer took place in the enclosure of the monastery but on the broad highways of the world.

However we must recognize that from our modern viewpoint there are a series of mistakes or lacks in the concept of action contained in the Exercises, which contributed to the growing split in the modern Christian consciousness.

1. The 'examination of conscience' for the first week is superficial in that it deals only with the 'individual conscience' in its monologue. Ricoeur severely criticises the superficiality of Descartes' *cogito* enclosed within itself, showing, as psychoanalysis and modern sociology of knowledge have proved,[19] that this is an 'appearance loaded with false images of the ego and false collective ideologies'. Exactly the same point could be made about the Ignatian *cogito* for the first week. We have a strong empirical proof of this: there was an 'inflation of Ignatian Exercises' [20] in the triumphalist principles of Franco's Fascism. Hundreds of thousands of young people and adults in the dominant élite which had won the civil war not only did the Exercises, but assiduously practiced the 'particular examination' of the individual *cogito*. But we do not know of a single case of anyone who discovered the depths of falsehood in his own self-awareness by means of this practice. Not one of these Christians who followed the Exercises discovered the tremendous contradiction (to Christianity) in prisons still full of ideological prisoners and a proletariat bitterly exploited and

silenced by ferocious political repression. This is natural: a monologue with one's own self-awareness is incapable of realizing its own radically false ideology.

2. The individualism of the model of action and decision proposed at the crucial point of the Exercises is determined by the radical insufficiency of the 'three moments of choice'.[21] The fourth is lacking! viz., deliberation by means of dialogue with brothers in the community. Of course there is an exact isomorphism between this way of thinking—which eliminates dialogue from action—and the dominant vertical juridical structure of the hierarchical Church of the Middle Ages. Thus there is the danger that the religious superior who has been through the 'three moments of choice' and stand alone 'before the sanctuary' convinced that he is 'inspired by God' will refuse to take into account all the work of a community assembly of any kind or the advice of experts. In fact modern psychology has shown us that the superior who does not really engage in dialogue with others, that is to say really involves them in the decision-making rather than merely consulting them, only encounters in the sanctuary the unconscious projection of his own wishes.[22]

After the Second World War, a method called 'life revision' was developed as a way of trying to rediscover a practical theory of Christian action. Life revision has certain values which are not to be found in the Exercises: (a) community dialogue; (b) it starts from real engagement in action; (c) it tries to apply the traditional 'discernment of spirits' in a concrete hermeneutics of historical praxis and the 'signs of the times'.

Life revision had its heyday, especially in the Latin Catholic countries, during the fifties and sixties until 1968, a crucial year in which the 'apostolic movements', the chief supporters of life revision, disintegrated. From then onwards there was a crisis which our pastoral thinking has not yet come to terms with. I think this has two possible reasons: (a) the ingenuous attempt at an immediate application to the analysis of real action (social, political, etc.) of a revision based on a 'fundamentalist' interpretation of the gospels. Committed militants rapidly discovered the need for other more scientific methods of analysis; (b) the principal failure was that of Catholic theologians, who remained enclosed within their pre-Vatican II speculations and were unable to provide a serious theological infrastructure to the practice of life revision.

This of course brings us back to the broader problem of the split in Christian consciousness. There is an enormous gap between the languages of faith (dogmatic, catechumenal, etc.) and the languages expressing the practice of modern action. While Christians remained in the defensive ecclesiastical ghetto of the nineteenth and twentieth centuries (Gregory XVI–Vatican II), there were no problems. But now when believers have at last taken their rightful place as the creative impetus in historical vanguards, they discover that the Spirit has no language.

OPENNESS TO THE SPIRIT OR RETURN TO A NEW DEFENSIVE LEGALITY?

One of the results of Vatican II was an 'opening of windows' to let in fresh air, although what blew in—according to one ecclesiastic—was a hurricane. Let us not forget that the Spirit has always been the mighty rushing wind of God's creative power.

We have to realize that for a superficial observer the real crisis of civilization is paralleled by profound crisis in the Church.[23] There can be two interpretations of this: the Catholic Church is dissolving with the fall of the bastion of authority and institutional authority in the West. And curiously this is in fact the interpretation given by some 'right-wing atheists', like Raymond Aron,[24] who recalls the attitude of Charles Maurras. Or the Church has opened the door to its spiritual power, previously repressed. In this case, amid the creative disorder of many different movements and tendencies, the Church is recovering its essential function, that of being a sign of hope in a world otherwise covered in darkness.

In this situation of crisis and creation we rediscover the decisive importance of two functional charismata of the Church. First the theological charisma. Will theologians be capable, after three centuries of speaking a different language, of entering again into dialogue with the culture and thought of today, which is also in crisis but powerfully creative? An enormous effort is required: to help invent new languages of faith, whose creative syntax retains its basic reference to the Gospel. Furthermore they must do this work while remaining in continuous dialogue with the base, because that is where, in the turmoil of everyday life, the Spirit moves, not on the hierarchical heights.

The other charisma is pastoral. It holds the key to the final alternative: to open or close the door to the Spirit.[25] Although we have not lost hope, we observe with dismay in the clarity given us by our intelligence of the faith, a slow movement back towards the vast hierarchical machinery, to judge by these symptoms:

1. There are clear signs of fear or reversion, especially at the highest levels of the Church. Slowly decisions of great assemblies are being annulled or an attempt is being made to direct or control them from the top.

2. Vatican II, in spite of its theological redefinition of the Church as sacrament and community, was unable to transform the solid ecclesiastical structure of the absolute accumulation of power in the head, which continues to rule this enormous Catholic society, with the incredible anachronism of a mediaeval model of absolute power, which is neither truly shared nor limited by the base.

3. All sociology and history agrees that what is most opposed to bureaucracy is the Creator Spirit.

4. Paul VI did not have the courage to take the decisive step and radically change the way of appointing a new pope and so the old system, even though it is medieval, or derived from obscure oriental despotisms could always co-opt from within a closed power group which thus perpetuates itself.

Notes

1. H. de Lubac, *Histoire et Esprit* (Paris, 1950); A. Carnap, *Fundamentale Theologie der Heilsgeschichte. Mysterium Salutis* I (Cologne, 1965), pp. 17–154; W. Kasper, *Glaube und Geschichte* (Düsseldorf, 1972); M. D. Chenu, *L'Evangile dans le temps* (Paris, 1960); J. B. Metz, J. Moltmann, & W. Oemüller, *Kirche im Prozess der Aufklärung* (Munich, 1970); R. Mate, *El ateismo como problema politico* (Salamanca, 1973); H. Fries, *Wandel des Kirchenbildes und dogmengeschichliche Entfaltung. Mysterium Salutis*, 4/1 (Cologne, 1972), pp. 223–80.

2. Cor. 11:28; 2 Cor. 13:5; Gal. 6:4:1 Th. 5:21ff.

3. Gal. 5:16–26; Rom. 8:14–16ff.

4. Rom. 13:8–10.

5. 1 Cor. 1:17–31.

6. 1 Cor. 12:13 and 14.

7. 1 Cor. 12:4–6.

8. The three estates, clergy, nobility and working people, revived in the politico-sacral ideology of the Middle Ages, have their roots in Indo-European prehistory. G. Dumezil, *Mythe et épopée. L'idéologie des trois fonctions dans les épopées des peuples indo-européens* (Paris, 1968). A stoic ideology of cosmic order reflected in social order, and a neo-Platonic vertically descending ideology legitimate the 'order' of domination: J. Le Golf, 'La Societé: les trois ordres et les exclus', in: *La civilisation de l'Occident Mediéval* (Paris, 1967). For H. Meyer the central idea in St Thomas, the perfect exponent of ecclesial ideology, is based on this idea of hierarchical order. See 'Die Welt, ein Ordo', in: *Thomas von Aquin. Sein System und seine geschichtliche Stellung* (Paderborn, 1961). The theoretical foundation of his treatise on obedience (2–2, q. 104, a. 1 corpus), which is the basic political ethic of the people under the *'princeps'*, derives from a neo-Platonic ideology of a natural and social cosmos

ordered in a vertically descending hierarchy.

9. G. Ostrogorsky, *Geschichte des Byzantinischen Staates* (Munich, 1952); A. Alfoldi, *Die Ausgestaltung des monarquischen Zeremoniellen am Romische Kaiserhöfe*, Deutschen Arch. Inst. Rom. Abt. 49 (1934), pp. 1–118.

10. This is a vast subject. We note merely three key works: M. Arquilliere, *L'Augustinisme politique* (Paris, 1955); M. Pacault, *La Théocratie. L'Eglise et le pouvoir au moyen âge* (Paris, 1957); W. Ullman, *Principles of Government and Politics in the Middle Ages* (London, 1961).

11. *Gaudium et Spes*, 36.

12. G. W. F. Hegel, *Glauben und Wissen* (Hamburg, 1962); idem, *Phänomenologie des Geistes. Das unglückliche Bewusstsein* (Hamburg, 1952), p. 158ff.

13. Several viewpoints on a complex problem: N. Cohn, *The Pursuit of the Millennium* (London, 1961); G. Fourquin, *Les soulèvements populaires au moyen âge* (Paris, 1972); H. Maisonneuve, *Etudes sur les origines de l'Inquisition* (Paris, 1960).

14. A classic model: St. Thomas Aquinas, *De Regimine principum* (Rome, 1948).

15. In the sense of a movement which transcends itself.

16. There is an important line of Catholic philosophers who begin with Thomism and bravely incorporate Kantian thought: Marechal, Rahner, Coreth, De Finance, Lonergan and the Spanish philosopher J. Gomez Caffarena, in his magnificent trilogy *Metafisica Fundamental* (Madrid, 1969), *Metafisica Transcendental* (Madrid, 1970) and together with Martin Velasco, *Filosofia de la religion* (Madrid, 1973).

17. In the sense in which Kühn uses this word in his work, *The Structure of Scientific Revolutions* (Chicago, 1962).

18. This is the line towards which conciliar reflections tend after Vatican II, beginning with *Mysterium Salutis*.

19. Cf. P. Ricoeur, *Le conflit des interpretations. Essai d'hermeneutique* (Paris, 1969), pp. 21–22.

20. F. Urbina, C. Marti and others, *Iglesia y sociedad en España 1939–1975* (Madrid, 1977). For the Spiritual Exercises see pp. 21–26.

21. *Ejercicios*, n. 175, BAC edition, Madrid, p. 194.

22. However I do not mean by this criticism to deny the value of a method, which purified from its historical limitations, can still be a great help today to people who want meditation, prayer and critical confrontation with the Gospel.

23. The literature on this is enormous. I mention only two examples by intelligent authors: J. L. L. Aranguren, *La crisis del catolicismo* (Madrid, 1970); M. de Certeau, J. M. Domenach, *Le christianisme éclaté* (Paris, 1974).

24. R. Aron, *Plaidoyer pour l'Europe décadent* (Paris, 1977).

25. Do not quench the Spirit! 1 Th. 5:19.

Contributors

JOSEP ROVIRA BELLOSO is professor of systematic theology in the Theology Faculty of Barcelona University, Spain. He has published in Catalan on faith and freedom, and a major analytical study of the Council of Trent.

JOSE CASTILLO is professor of dogmatic theology in the Theological Faculty of Granada University, Spain. He has been visiting professor in Madrid and at the Gregorian in Rome. He has published on prayer, Christian life, Christian discernment in St Paul, and the Church of the people.

YVES CONGAR, O.P., is a member of the International Theological Commission. Among his many works are studies of tradition and traditions, mediaeval ecclesiology, St Augustine in the modern age, the Church, ministry and communion, salvation and liberation, and the Church in modern France.

ENRIQUE DUSSEL is professor at the Autonomous University of Mexico and in the Religious Sciences Department of the Iberoamerican University. He is chairperson of the Study Commission of the Church in Latin America (CEHILA). He has published widely on liberation theology, Latin-American church history, and ethical philosophy.

MARTIN MC NAMARA is professor of sacred Scripture and dean of theology at the Milltown Institute of Theology and Philosophy, Dublin,

Ireland. He has published widely on scriptural topics, mainly on the prophets, on the Aramaic of NT Palestine, and on the Bible in the Irish Church.

CASIMIR MARTI is professor in the Theological Faculty of the University of Barcelona, Spain and a suburban pastor. He has published on the origins of anarchism in Barcelona, and the progressive and working-class movements in Barcelona.

WILLIAM PETERS, S.J., has published important studies of the poetry of Gerard Manley Hopkins and his Jesuit influences, and of the Spiritual Exercises of St Ignatius. Since Vatican II he has conducted the Spiritual Exercises of thirty days for priests and superiors in various parts of the world.

RENÉ SIMON, S.D.B., was until his retirement in 1977 professor of moral theology at the Catholic Institute in Paris and also taught at the Catholic Theological Faculty in Strasbourg, France. He has published extensively on ethics, moral philosophy, dialectics of faith, and spirituality.

JON SOBRINO, S.J., is professor of theology in the Central American University of José Simeón Cañas in San Salvador, El Salvador. He has published on Christology in Latin America and on the clergy and the third world.

FERNANDO URBINA is a diocesan priest in Madrid. He is superior at the Hispano-American Seminary in Madrid, and professor of fundamental theology at the Madrid Seminary. He is the editor of the review *Pastoral Misionera*. He has published on violence and the Church, missions, the priesthood, and the Church in Spain.

ENRIQUE M. UREÑA, S.J., is professor of social theory and philosophy of religion at the Comillas University in Madrid. He has published on Marx, economics, Freud and social theory, Habermas, and Kantian social theory.